INTRODUCING
ISSUES WITH
OPPOSING
VIEWPOINTS®

T4-AJT-895

Executive Privilege and the Powers of the Presidency

M. M. Eboch, Book Editor

GREENHAVEN
PUBLISHING

Published in 2022 by Greenhaven Publishing, LLC
353 3rd Avenue, Suite 255, New York, NY 10010

Articles in Greenhaven Publishing anthologies are often edited for length to meet page requirements. In addition, original titles of these works are changed to clearly present the main thesis and to explicitly indicate the author's opinion. Every effort is made to ensure that Greenhaven Publishing accurately reflects the original intent of the authors. Every effort has been made to trace the owners of the copyrighted material.

Library of Congress Cataloging-in-Publication Data

Names: Eboch, M. M., editor.
Title: Executive privilege and the powers of the presidency / M. M. Eboch,
    book editor.
Description: First edition. | New York : Greenhaven Publishing, 2022. |
    Series: Introducing issues with opposing viewpoints | Includes
    bibliographical references and index. | Contents: Executive privilege
    and the powers of the presidency | Audience: Ages 12–15 | Audience: Grades 7–9 |
    Summary: "Anthology of curated viewpoints in which experts make their cases both against
    and in support of executive privilege and project how it might be
    expanded or limited in the future."— Provided by publisher.
Identifiers: LCCN 2020049269 | ISBN 9781534507975 (library binding) | ISBN
    9781534507968 (paperback)
Subjects: LCSH: Executive privilege (Government information)—United
    States—Juvenile literature. | Executive power—United States—Juvenile
    literature. | Presidents—United States—Juvenile literature.
Classification: LCC KF4570 .E94 2022 | DDC 346.73/06—dc23
LC record available at https://lccn.loc.gov/2020049269

Manufactured in the United States of America

Website: http://greenhavenpublishing.com

Contents

Foreword

Indulging in a wide spectrum of ideas, beliefs, and perspectives is a critical cornerstone of democracy. After all, it is often debates over differences of opinion, such as whether to legalize abortion, how to treat prisoners, or when to enact the death penalty, that shape our society and drive it forward. Such diversity of thought is frequently regarded as the hallmark of a healthy and civilized culture. As the Reverend Clifford Schutjer of the First Congregational Church in Mansfield, Ohio, declared in a 2001 sermon, "Surrounding oneself with only like-minded people, restricting what we listen to or read only to what we find agreeable is irresponsible. Refusing to entertain doubts once we make up our minds is a subtle but deadly form of arrogance." With this advice in mind, Introducing Issues with Opposing Viewpoints books aim to open readers' minds to the critically divergent views that comprise our world's most important debates.

Introducing Issues with Opposing Viewpoints simplifies for students the enormous and often overwhelming mass of material now available via print and electronic media. Collected in every volume is an array of opinions that captures the essence of a particular controversy or topic. Introducing Issues with Opposing Viewpoints books embody the spirit of nineteenth-century journalist Charles A. Dana's axiom: "Fight for your opinions, but do not believe that they contain the whole truth, or the only truth." Absorbing such contrasting opinions teaches students to analyze the strength of an argument and compare it to its opposition. From this process readers can inform and strengthen their own opinions or be exposed to new information that will change their minds. Introducing Issues with Opposing Viewpoints is a mosaic of different voices. The authors are statesmen, pundits, academics, journalists, corporations, and ordinary people who have felt compelled to share their experiences and ideas in a public forum. Their words have been collected from newspapers, journals, books, speeches, interviews, and the internet, the fastest growing body of opinionated material in the world.

Introducing Issues with Opposing Viewpoints shares many of the well-known features of its critically acclaimed parent series, Opposing Viewpoints. The articles allow readers to absorb and compare divergent perspectives. Active reading questions preface each viewpoint, requiring the student to approach the material thoughtfully and carefully. Photographs, charts, and graphs supplement each article. A thorough introduction provides readers with crucial background on an issue. An annotated bibliography points the reader toward articles, books, and websites that contain additional information on the topic. An appendix of organizations to contact contains a wide variety of charities, nonprofit organizations, political groups, and private enterprises that each hold a position on the issue at hand. Finally, a comprehensive index allows readers to locate content quickly and efficiently.

Introducing Issues with Opposing Viewpoints is also significantly different from Opposing Viewpoints. As the series title implies, its presentation will help introduce students to the concept of opposing viewpoints and learn to use this material to aid in critical writing and debate. The series' four-color, accessible format makes the books attractive and inviting to readers of all levels. In addition, each viewpoint has been carefully edited to maximize a reader's understanding of the content. Short but thorough viewpoints capture the essence of an argument. A substantial, thought-provoking essay question placed at the end of each viewpoint asks the student to further investigate the issues raised in the viewpoint, compare and contrast two authors' arguments, or consider how one might go about forming an opinion on the topic at hand. Each viewpoint contains sidebars that include at-a-glance information and handy statistics. A Facts About section located in the back of the book further supplies students with relevant facts and figures.

Following in the tradition of the Opposing Viewpoints series, Greenhaven Publishing continues to provide readers with invaluable exposure to the controversial issues that shape our world. As John Stuart Mill once wrote: "The only way in which a human being can make some approach to knowing the whole of a subject is by hearing what can be said about it by persons of every variety of opinion and studying all modes in which it can be looked at by every character of mind. No wise man ever acquired his wisdom in any mode but this." It is to this principle that Introducing Issues with Opposing Viewpoints books are dedicated.

Introduction

"After the last Senate staffer turns out the lights, major questions remain to be decided outside of the Capitol about the limits of presidential power, the willingness of courts to decide political questions and the ability of Congress to exercise effective oversight and hold a president accountable."
—Barbara L. McQuade

Is the US president the most powerful person in the country, perhaps even the world? Many people would say yes. In reality, US presidents are limited in what they can do on their own. They must work with a variety of politicians and government agencies to gain support for their programs and to pass laws. If they don't have support from the general public as well, the president might lose the next election or cause fallout for their political party.

Still, there's no doubt that the US president has great power. The powers and duties of the president are laid out in the Constitution. Article II of the US Constitution tries to balance the powers of the three branches of government: the executive (the president and about 5 million workers), legislative (Senate and House of Representatives), and judicial (Supreme Court and lower courts). The drafters of the Constitution wanted to make sure no branch could become overly powerful.

Article I of the US Constitution describes the powers given to Congress, including the power to make laws. The courts have agreed that this means Congress has the power to conduct investigations as needed in order to uphold the laws. At times, that may include investigating the actions of a president. If Congress believes the president has committed illegal acts, whether misdemeanors or treason, then Congress can attempt to remove the president from office through the process of impeachment.

To impeach a president, the House of Representatives first sets up a committee to investigate. The House determines any charges against the president and votes on those charges. If a majority agrees with the charges, the case goes to the Senate. The Senate can go to trial or vote to dismiss the charges. In a trial, a two-thirds majority must vote for impeachment in order to convict the president.

In order to make rational legal decisions in an impeachment case, Congress needs accurate and detailed information about the president's behavior. On the other hand, the president has certain rights to privacy. These competing claims may come into conflict.

The Constitution does not use the term "executive privilege." However, throughout the history of the United States, presidents have claimed the right to keep certain documents and conversations private. The courts have agreed, but only in certain circumstances, such as secrets related to national security, the military, or diplomatic relations. This helps protect the country by, for example, not broadcasting information about military readiness or plans to fight terrorism.

The situation gets trickier when it comes to discussions on other topics. Some experts claim all the president's discussions with advisers may be privileged, and thus kept secret, in order to allow the free and open sharing of ideas. In *United States v. Nixon*, decided in 1974, the Supreme Court noted, "Human experience teaches that those who expect public dissemination of their remarks may well temper candor with a concern for appearances and for their own interests to the detriment of the decision-making process." In other words, if people fear punishment for sharing ideas, they may not brainstorm as openly.

On the other hand, some experts argue that the president's advisers should know they may be called to testify in front of Congress. That way, they are pressured to only give advice that is legal. Allowing secret discussions could permit the president and advisers to collude on illegal actions.

In the case against President Nixon, the Supreme Court acknowledged the need for private communications between government officials and their aides. However, the Court said a president's claim to executive privilege is not absolute. Instead, the judicial branch must be able to access information it needs in order to uphold the law. In particular, the court has the right to information needed to consider criminal cases, including impeachment trials.

There is also the question of how far executive privilege extends. It is typically seen to cover the president and close advisers. But does it cover all advisers? Does it cover discussions or written communications that never reached the president?

During the presidency of George W. Bush (2001–2009), the DC District Court rejected the idea that presidential aides have absolute immunity. The judge noted that executive privilege might allow an aide to refuse to answer specific questions. It did not exempt them from testifying altogether.

Many presidents and presidential aides have claimed executive privilege to avoid testifying. Typically, Congress and the president then negotiate what information can be discussed. In other cases, the standoff has continued until the information is no longer important, so the issue is dropped. When cases go to the courts, the findings may only apply in certain narrow circumstances. This makes it difficult to say definitely when executive privilege applies. Each president may test the law in new ways.

In 2017, Congress appointed a special counsel to investigate President Donald Trump. The investigation looked into links between Russia and the Trump presidential campaign, including charges that the Russian government had interfered in the 2016 election. To carry out the investigation, Congress asked many presidential aides to testify. President Trump ordered them not to testify, and most refused to speak to Congress on any topic, claiming executive privilege.

Opponents argued that President Trump tried to take executive privilege too far and obstructed justice. As with previous impeachment cases, the argument broke down along party lines. Many Republicans supported the Republican president, while Democrats pushed for impeachment. The Democratic-led House of Representatives passed a vote for impeachment. In the Senate, every Democrat voted for impeachment. Every Republican voted to acquit the president, except for one who split his vote on the two charges. The Senate didn't have the two-thirds majority needed to impeach.

Executive privilege is a complex legal concept. It is important that the general public understand it in order to follow what happens during impeachment trials. The current debates are explored by experts in the field in the viewpoints that make up *Introducing Issues with Opposing Viewpoints: Executive Privilege and the Powers of the Presidency*, shedding light on this ongoing contemporary issue.

Chapter 1

How and Why Does Executive Privilege Give the President Power?

The US presidency has become more powerful than the Founding Fathers intended.

Executive Privilege Has Limits

Robert Longley

"For their advisers to be open and candid in giving advice, they must feel safe that the discussions will remain confidential."

In the following viewpoint, Robert Longley argues that executive privilege has not been legally defined in detail, but typically it assumes that the president may have reasons for keeping secrets related to his or her written and spoken communications in certain circumstances. Discussions with advisers may be privileged, and thus kept secret, in order to allow the free and open sharing of ideas. Secrets related to national security, the military, or diplomatic relations may fall under the category of privileged communications. Robert Longley is a history and government writer.

"Presidential Executive Privilege," by Robert Longley, ThoughtCo, December 4, 2018. Reprinted by permission.

AS YOU READ, CONSIDER THE FOLLOWING QUESTIONS:
1. What is executive privilege?
2. Does executive privilege mean the president can keep all communications private?
3. What are the main categories that fall under executive privilege?

Executive privilege is an implied power claimed by Presidents of the United States and other officials of the executive branch of government to withhold from Congress, the courts or individuals, information that has been requested or subpoenaed. Executive privilege is also invoked to prevent executive branch employees or officials from testifying in Congressional hearings.

The US Constitution makes no mention of either the power of Congress or the federal courts to request information or the concept of an executive privilege to refuse such requests. However, the US Supreme Court has ruled that executive privilege may be a legitimate aspect of the separation of powers doctrine, based on the constitutional powers of the executive branch to manage its own activities.

In the case of *United States v. Nixon*, the Supreme Court upheld the doctrine of executive privilege in the case of subpoenas for information issued by the judicial branch, instead of by Congress. In the court's majority opinion, Chief Justice Warren Burger wrote that the president holds a qualified privilege to require that the party seeking certain documents must make a "sufficient showing" that the "Presidential material" is "essential to the justice of the case." Justice Berger also stated that the president's executive privilege would more likely to be valid when applied to cases when the oversight of the executive would impair that the executive branch's ability to address concerns of national security.

Reasons for Claiming Executive Privilege

Historically, presidents have exercised executive privilege in two types of cases: those that involve national security and those that involve executive branch communications.

The courts have ruled that presidents can also exercise executive privilege in cases involving ongoing investigations by law enforcement

Congress has never succeeded in passing legislation that would clearly define and possibly limit executive privilege.

or during deliberations involving disclosure or discovery in civil litigation involving the federal government.

Just as Congress must prove it has the right to investigate, the executive branch must prove it has a valid reason to withhold information.

While there have been efforts in Congress to pass laws clearly defining executive privilege and setting guidelines for its use, no such legislation has ever passed and none is likely to do so in the future.

Reasons of National Security

Presidents most often claim executive privilege to protect sensitive military or diplomatic information, which if disclosed, could place the security of the United States at risk. Given the president's constitutional power as commander and chief of the US Military, this "state secrets" claim of executive privilege is rarely challenged.

Reasons of Executive Branch Communications

Most conversations between presidents and their top aides and advisers are transcribed or electronically recorded. Presidents have contended that executive privilege secrecy should be extended to the records of some of those conversations. The presidents argue that in order for their advisers to be open and candid in giving advice, and to present all possible ideas, they must feel safe that the discussions will remain confidential. This application of executive privilege, while rare, is always controversial and often challenged.

In the 1974 Supreme Court case of *United States v. Nixon*, the Court acknowledged "the valid need for protection of communications between high Government officials and those who advise and assist them in the performance of their manifold duties." The Court went on to state that "[h]uman experience teaches that those who expect public dissemination of their remarks may well temper candor with a concern for appearances and for their own interests to the detriment of the decision-making process."

While the Court thus conceded the need for confidentiality in discussions between presidents and their advisers, it ruled that the right of presidents to keep those discussions secret under a claim of executive privilege was not absolute, and could be overturned by a judge. In the Court's majority opinion, Chief Justice Warren Burger wrote, "[n]either the doctrine of separation of powers, nor the need for confidentiality of high-level communications, without more, can sustain an absolute, unqualified Presidential privilege of immunity from judicial process under all circumstances."

The ruling reaffirmed decisions from earlier Supreme Court cases, including *Marbury v. Madison*, establishing that the US court system is the final decider of constitutional questions and that no person, not even the president of the United States, is above the law.

Brief History of Executive Privilege

While Dwight D. Eisenhower was the first president to actually use the phrase "executive privilege," every president since George Washington has exercised some form of the power.

In 1792, Congress demanded information from President Washington regarding a failed US military expedition. Along with records about the operation, Congress called members of the White House staff to appear and deliver sworn testimony. With the advice and consent of his Cabinet, Washington decided that, as the chief executive, he had the authority to withhold information from Congress. Although he eventually decided to cooperate with Congress, Washington built the foundation for future use of executive privilege.

Indeed, George Washington set the proper and now recognized standard for using executive privilege: Presidential secrecy must be exercised only when it serves the public interest.

EVALUATING THE AUTHOR'S ARGUMENTS:

Viewpoint author Robert Longley explains the privileges and limitations exercised by the US presidency. Does the author's viewpoint give you the impression that it seems reasonable that the president should be able to keep certain communications secret? Why or why not, and under what conditions?

Impeachment Could Be Avoided with Executive Privilege

"They just don't have to show up, and they don't have to provide the testimony that's been demanded or subpoenaed from Congress."

NPR

In the following viewpoint, National Public Radio (NPR) explores how President Trump might have used the concept of executive privilege to limit the information presented in the 2019 impeachment hearings against him. The executive branch insisted that Congress does not have the authority to force the president to testify and that close aides to the president are immune from congressional subpoenas that would force them to testify. This concept has not been legally proven, but testing the concept in a court case could take years. NPR is a nonprofit media organization.

NPR's Ailsa Chang speaks with Jonathan Shaub, a former US Department of Justice legal adviser, about how the Trump administration is stymieing impeachment hearings with legally untested doctrine.

AILSA CHANG, HOST:

In Washington, it is a daily guessing game on whether or not key witnesses will testify in the House's impeachment inquiry. That's because of the push and pull between the Trump administration telling aides not to speak and Congress issuing them subpoenas, saying they have to appear. Just this afternoon, the White House indicated it will not permit acting Chief of Staff Mick Mulvaney to testify. But if it comes to it, could the president invoke what's called executive privilege to stop high-level witnesses from testifying?

Well, to help us answer that question, I'm joined now by Jonathan Shaub. He served in the US Department of Justice as recently as 2017.

Welcome.

JONATHAN SHAUB: Thank you.

CHANG: OK. Let's just have you start out by briefly defining for us—what is executive privilege?

SHAUB: Executive privilege is a—it's a constitutional doctrine that says the president can withhold sensitive information from Congress or from the courts when it's necessary to protect the public interest.

CHANG: OK. So what might President Trump's argument be if he were to use executive privilege to not cooperate in this impeachment inquiry?

SHAUB: Generally, the executive branch view is that there are certain kinds of information, such as the conversations of the president or national security information or, here, there's some diplomatic negotiations. And the view is that these are confidential and shouldn't be disclosed unless absolutely necessary. And so I think the argument would be this information is very sensitive, and Congress doesn't really need it because, you know, we've released other information. And so the president is going to withhold it and assert executive privilege.

CHANG: And so far, President Trump has not yet explicitly asserted executive privilege during these impeachment proceedings. Correct?

SHAUB: Correct, right.

CHANG: OK. But just to be clear, as a matter of law, like, no communication involving the White House enjoys absolute immunity. Right? There's no blanket immunity out there.

SHAUB: Right, not for communications. The executive privilege is a qualified privilege. So the Supreme Court, in the Nixon case, with the Watergate tapes, said there is a presumption that the tapes are privileged and the conversations of the president are privileged, but if there is a need for it, then that can overcome that presumption. And in that case, it found that the grand jury needed the tapes in order to sort of assess what had happened.

President Trump's acting chief of staff, Mick Mulvaney (right), refused a subpoena to testify in House impeachment inquiries in 2019, claiming absolute immunity.

CHANG: If President Trump were not to use executive privilege, are there any other legal claims of immunity out there that President Trump could theoretically rely on to, say, stop people in his administration from testifying?

SHAUB: Yes, and he has. He's asserted what we think of as testimonial immunity for close presidential aides.

CHANG: What is that?

SHAUB: The idea is Congress and the president are sort of co-equal branches. And Congress, in the executive branch's view, at least, doesn't have the authority to subpoena the president and force him to come testify. And his close aides are sort of alter egos of the president. Since about 1970 or so, the executive branch has really developed this idea that close presidential advisers can't be compelled to testify before Congress. They're immune from those subpoenas that are issued.

And it's broader than privilege because it's not qualified.

CHANG: Meaning there's no limits to it.

SHAUB: Right. They just don't have to show up, and they don't have to provide the information, the testimony that's been demanded or subpoenaed from Congress.

CHANG: So what is the best check on Congress if lawmakers were to overreach in their oversight role?

SHAUB: Checks on Congress traditionally have been this compromise and this accommodation process, where the executive branch says, look. These are really sensitive things; we'll try to take that into account and get just the information we need and respect those interests. I think that compromise and the sort of normative approach has broken down. And at this point, there's not a real way to resolve it until you have a court decision that says, this is what the Constitution means and this is where the authority is—because the executive branch has a number of doctrines, like executive privilege and immunity to refuse to comply if Congress is not going to respect those confidentiality interests.

Now, whether those apply in impeachment is sort of an unsettled question. And going forward, I think we're likely to see some challenges on that basis.

CHANG: Jonathan Shaub is also currently the Tennessee assistant solicitor general.
Thank you very much for joining us.

SHAUB: Thanks for having me.

EVALUATING THE AUTHOR'S ARGUMENTS:

In this viewpoint, Jonathan Shaub contends that the president does not enjoy absolute privilege or immunity. Do you think that the standard is adequately set in the US Constitution? Why or why not? How might the rules change, depending on the situation?

Viewpoint 3

There Is Remarkably Little Case Law on Executive Privilege

Steve Vladeck

"[T]he Supreme Court has never addressed executive privilege in the face of a congressional demand for information."

In the following viewpoint, Steve Vladeck argues that the Supreme Court recognized executive privilege in a case against President Richard Nixon, citing the need for private communications between government officials and their aides. However, the Court said a president's claim to executive privilege is not absolute. Instead, the judicial branch must be able to access information it needs in order to uphold the law. In particular, the Court has the right to information needed to consider a criminal case. Steve Vladeck is a professor of law at the University of Texas School of Law.

"Executive Privilege, Congress' Subpoena Power, and the Courts: A Brief Overview of a Complex Topic," by Steve Vladeck, US Supreme Court, October 16, 2019. Reprinted by permission.

AS YOU READ, CONSIDER THE FOLLOWING QUESTIONS:

1. Why has the concept of executive privilege not been challenged in court very much?
2. How did President Trump's presidency show the shortcomings of using negotiation to decide who would testify?
3. How did a court challenge to President Nixon affect the future of executive privilege?

As much as it is discussed and debated, especially lately, there is remarkably little case law concerning "executive privilege"—the idea that there are at least some internal executive branch communications that are shielded against compelled disclosure. The Supreme Court has decided exactly one case involving the privilege, and even that decision—in the Watergate tapes case, *United States v. Nixon*—raised as many questions as it answered. One reason courts have historically had so little to say about the privilege is because, as the Congressional Research Service explained in 2014, "[t]he vast majority of these disputes are resolved through political negotiation and accommodation." Most privilege claims arise in disputes between Congress and the executive branch, and most of the time, the involved parties are able to reach some kind of compromise—or the relevant administration and/or Congress ends—before the dispute is conclusively settled by the courts. That's why the most voluminous discussions of executive privilege have come in memoranda by the Justice Department's Office of Legal Counsel—rather than judicial decisions.

But "political negotiation and accommodation" have not exactly characterized the relationship between the Trump administration and the House of Representatives over the past nine months. As a growing list of witnesses have refused to appear before Congress or turn over requested documents, the House has issued a steadily increasing number of subpoenas, which has in turn provoked litigation over the scope of Congress' subpoena power and, in some circumstances, whether and to what extent executive privilege provides a defense even against duly issued subpoenas. Last Friday, a divided panel of the US Court of Appeals for the D.C. Circuit decided the first of these disputes, holding that President Donald Trump could not block one of his accounting firms from complying with a subpoena for financial records in the firm's possession because the subpoena was within Congress' authority to issue. And that ruling came on the heels of an eye-opening letter sent last Tuesday by White House Counsel Pat Cipollone to House Speaker Nancy Pelosi and three House committee chairs, suggesting that the White House will not comply with any information requests related to a potential impeachment inquiry.

For now, at least, these disputes are pitched at a categorical level. If and when courts reach specific claims of executive privilege, they'll find some clarity, but also a series of open questions, in the relevant case law. The following post tries to clarify what's been settled and what hasn't.

1. The Supreme Court and Executive Privilege

As the 2014 CRS study explained, "the Supreme Court has never addressed executive privilege in the face of a congressional demand for information." Instead, the case in which the court first recognized such a privilege—Nixon—arose from a subpoena issued by Special Prosecutor Leon Jaworski as part of his investigation into the Watergate break-in. But the court's 8-0 ruling in *Nixon* nevertheless provides three important benchmarks for executive privilege vis-à-vis Congress today.

First, emphasizing "the valid need for protection of communications between high Government officials and those who advise and assist them in the performance of their manifold duties," the Nixon court traced executive privilege not to the common law, but to Article II of the Constitution. As Chief Justice Warren Burger wrote, "[w]hatever the nature of the privilege of confidentiality of Presidential communications in the exercise of Art[icle] II powers, the privilege can be said to derive from the supremacy of each branch within its own assigned area of constitutional duties." In other words, "the protection of the confidentiality of Presidential communications has … constitutional underpinnings," meaning that the privilege cannot be abrogated by statute. Indeed, even though President Richard Nixon ultimately lost before the court, this part of the court's decision was a significant (and, given the result, unnecessary) win for the presidency.

The Supreme Court case involving President Richard Nixon's claims to executive privilege set important precedents.

Second, the *Nixon* court rejected the president's claim that such a privilege is absolute, emphasizing that "the impediment that an absolute, unqualified privilege would place in the way of the primary constitutional duty of the Judicial Branch to do justice in criminal prosecutions would plainly conflict with the function of the courts under Art[icle] III." Instead, the court held that the executive privilege protected by Article II is a qualified privilege, and concluded that "it is necessary to resolve [the] competing interests" between executive privilege and the role of the courts "in a manner that preserves the essential functions of each branch."

Third, *Nixon* held that the president's interest in the confidentiality of his own communications, as memorialized in the tapes sought by the subpoena, was outweighed by "our historic commitment to the rule of law." In *Nixon*, specifically, "when the ground for asserting privilege as to subpoenaed materials sought for use in a criminal trial is based only on the generalized interest in confidentiality, it cannot prevail over the fundamental demands of due process of law in the fair administration of criminal justice." And as the court would explain three years later in another case involving Nixon, the privilege recognized in the earlier 1974 *Nixon* ruling "is limited to communications 'in performance of (a President's) responsibilities … of his office,' and made 'in the process of shaping policies and making decisions.'"

2. The D.C. Circuit's Major Rulings:
Espy and *Judicial Watch*

Although the Supreme Court has not considered the scope of executive privilege since the 1970's, the D.C. Circuit has ruled on the issue several times. Two especially instructive decisions are the 1997 decision in *In re Sealed Case* (known to posterity as the *Espy* ruling); and the 2004 ruling in *Judicial Watch v. US Department of Justice*.

Espy concerns a grand jury subpoena for White House documents that arose out of a criminal investigation into former Secretary of Agriculture Mike Espy. In siding largely, but not entirely, with the White House, the D.C. Circuit clarified several features about executive privilege. First, as Judge Patricia Wald explained for the unanimous three-judge panel, executive privilege is, in fact, two different privileges: the "presidential communications privilege" recognized by the Supreme Court in *Nixon*, and a more general "deliberative process privilege," derived from the common law. As the court explained, the latter privilege covers most internal decisionmaking within the executive branch, but is far easier to overcome. The former privilege, in contrast, applies only to "direct decisionmaking by the President," and is far harder to overcome—requiring a greater showing of need by the requesting party, along with the unavailability of other mechanisms for obtaining similar evidence.

Espy also clarified that "communications made by presidential advisers in the course of preparing advice for the President come under the presidential communications privilege, even when these communications are not made directly to the President." To that end, "[t]he

privilege must also extend to communications authored or received in
response to a solicitation by members of a presidential adviser's staff,
since in many instances advisers
must rely on their staff to investigate
an issue and formulate the advice
to be given to the President." But
Espy also stressed that "the presidential communications privilege
should be construed as narrowly as

is consistent with ensuring that the confidentiality of the President's
decisionmaking process is adequately protected." Thus, "the privilege should not extend to staff outside the White House in executive
branch agencies." Instead, "the privilege should apply only to communications authored or solicited and received by those members of
an immediate White House adviser's staff who have broad and significant responsibility for investigating and formulating the advice to
be given the President on the particular matter to which the communications relate," and only when the communications are specifically
related to advice to the President "on official government matters."
As the court concluded, "[t]he presidential communications privilege should never serve as a means of shielding information regarding
governmental operations that do not call ultimately for direct decisionmaking by the President."

Seven years later, a different D.C. Circuit panel further sharpened
Espy's analysis in *Judicial Watch*, a Freedom of Information Act suit
seeking disclosure of DOJ documents relating to pardon applications
and pardon grants. The government asserted both the presidential
communications privilege and the deliberative process privilege as
grounds for withholding disclosure under FOIA. But the court of
appeals rejected the argument that the documents were protected by
the presidential communications privilege. As Judge Judith Rogers
wrote for a divided panel, even though the materials related to a
"quintessential and non-delegable Presidential power"—the power
to pardon—"internal agency documents that are not 'solicited and
received' by the President or his Office are instead protected against

disclosure, if at all, by the deliberative process privilege." Although *Espy* had, for the first time, expanded the presidential communications privilege to encompass communications not directly involving the president, *Judicial Watch* stressed the narrowness of that extension: "[W]hile 'communications authored or solicited and received' by immediate White House advisors in the Office of the President could qualify under the privilege, communications of staff outside the White House in executive branch agencies that were not solicited and received by such White House advisors could not."

Between them, *Espy* and *Judicial Watch* yield several conclusions about the scope of the presidential communications privilege under D.C. Circuit case law. First, the privilege may be asserted even as to communications in which the president is not personally involved. Second, the communications must nevertheless relate to "official government matters" calling for "direct decisionmaking by the President." Third, at most, the privilege can only be claimed by senior White House advisers (and their immediate staffers). Fourth, and most importantly, the scope of the privilege is to be construed as "narrowly" as is consistent with the confidentiality of the president's communications.

3. Judge John Bates' Ruling in *Miers*

Although district court decisions do not have the same precedential force as rulings by the Supreme Court and courts of appeals, one ruling from the US District Court for the District of Columbia subsequent to the D.C. Circuit's *Judicial Watch* decision may provide further insight into the scope of executive privilege today. In *House Committee on the Judiciary v. Miers*, Judge John Bates held that neither current nor former senior advisers to the president are absolutely immune from compelled congressional process—rejecting a claim that "executive privilege" protected the White House chief of staff or the former White House counsel from compliance with otherwise valid congressional subpoenas. In the process, Bates rejected the White House's argument that the Supreme Court's 1974 *Nixon* decision was limited to criminal subpoenas:

> *Congress's power of inquiry is as broad as its power to legislate and lies at the very heart of Congress's constitutional*

role. Indeed, the former is necessary to the proper exercise of the latter: according to the Supreme Court, the ability to compel testimony is "necessary to the effective functioning of courts and legislatures." Thus, Congress's use of (and need for vindication of) its subpoena power in this case is no less legitimate or important than was the grand jury's in United States v. Nixon. *Both involve core functions of a co-equal branch of the federal government, and for the reasons identified in* Nixon, *the President may only be entitled to a presumptive, rather than an absolute, privilege here. And it is certainly the case that if the President is entitled only to a presumptive privilege, his close advisors cannot hold the superior card of absolute immunity.*

The district court did not reach the merits of the privilege claim in *Miers*. And the government's appeal was voluntarily dismissed after the parties settled. But Bates' ruling stands as the only decision to date that expressly rejects an effort to distinguish the *Nixon* analysis as not applying to congressional subpoenas, and it rejects the argument that current or former senior White House advisors enjoy absolute testimonial immunity vis-à-vis Congress. If other courts follow Bates' lead, that would have significant ramifications for executive privilege claims against Congress going forward. Much remains unanswered by the courts, but the guidance from *Espy*, *Judicial Watch* and *Miers* should go a long way toward separating colorable privilege claims from those that are patently meritless.

4. Lessons for the Future

In its 1977 ruling in *United States v. AT&T Co.*, the D.C. Circuit refused to resolve a dispute between the DOJ and the House of Representatives arising out of a subpoena the House had issued to a private company for records that DOJ claimed were protected by executive privilege. As Judge Harold Leventhal wrote:

> *The framers … relied, we believe, on the expectation that where conflicts in scope of authority arose between the coordinate*

branches, a spirit of dynamic compromise would promote resolution of the dispute in the manner most likely to result in efficient and effective functioning of our governmental system. Under this view, the coordinate branches do not exist in an exclusively adversary relationship to one another when a conflict in authority arises. Rather, each branch should take cognizance of an implicit constitutional mandate to seek optimal accommodation through a realistic evaluation of the needs of the conflicting branches in the particular fact situation. This aspect of our constitutional scheme avoids the mischief of polarization of disputes.

For better or worse, our contemporary politics are beset with "the mischief of polarization of disputes." And as the D.C. Circuit suggested in *AT&T Co.*, the burden will eventually fall upon the courts to settle these disputes if, as seems increasingly likely, the political process cannot. However the courts ultimately resolve these cases, we should all bemoan the demise of the "spirit of dynamic compromise." It remains to be seen whether the courts will move quickly enough to prevent the current disputes from being mooted by the next election, which will return a new House of Representatives regardless of the results of the presidential election.

EVALUATING THE AUTHOR'S ARGUMENTS:

In this viewpoint, author Steve Vladeck asserts that the courts have not defined executive privilege in great detail, largely because they have not needed to. What are the risks of relying on case-by-case compromises instead of having clear rules about what counts as privilege communication?

Contempt of Congress Is One Option

Sarah D. Wire

"If convicted, the person is imprisoned until they agree to comply."

In the following viewpoint, Sarah D. Wire describes the battle between the different branches of government with regards to getting access to testimony in court. The author argues that in 2019, a Democrat-controlled Congress wanted people appointed by Republican President Trump to testify. The White House refused. The author explores some of the options Congress had and why they were challenging. Sarah D. Wire writes about Congress for the *Los Angeles Times*.

AS YOU READ, CONSIDER THE FOLLOWING QUESTIONS:
1. What happens if Congress finds someone in contempt?
2. Why is it challenging to hold someone from the executive branch in contempt, especially the attorney general?
3. How can impeachment be used when holding someone in contempt doesn't work?

Refusing to testify to Congress can result in a contempt charge. Such charges are rarely enforced against members of the executive branch.

A ngry that the Justice Department won't comply with a congressional subpoena for an unredacted version of special counsel Robert S. Mueller III's report, and frustrated by Atty. Gen. William Barr's decision to skip a hearing where he was to testify Thursday, the Democratic-controlled House is threatening to hold Barr in contempt.

It sets up a showdown over constitutional powers between the executive and legislative branches that President Trump and the House have built toward for months. Trump told reporters last week that he'll fight every subpoena. Here are some things you should know about what could happen next.

What Is Contempt of Congress?

A contempt finding is how Congress may respond when someone refuses to testify or provide information as part of a House or Senate investigation. The Supreme Court has repeatedly upheld that Congress has a right to compel people to comply with its oversight efforts.

Such demands are more complicated when they involve other branches of the government. Presidents always have information they don't want to give Congress. In the past, the mere threat of being held in contempt—not to mention Congress' power over funding the government—was usually enough to convince an administration to comply with a request, or at least negotiate a compromise.

Unlike impeachment proceedings, either chamber of Congress—the House or the Senate—can pursue contempt charges without needing the participation or approval of the other chamber.

How Common Is Contempt of Congress?

Not that common. Congress has found someone in contempt fewer than 30 times since 1980, according to the Congressional Research Service.

What Happens After Congress Holds Someone in Contempt?

Congress has a few options. The most common is that it can send a criminal contempt referral to a US attorney. If prosecuted and convicted, the punishment is up to a $10,000 fine and a year in jail.

But Will the Justice Department Enforce a Contempt of Congress Finding Against a Member of the Executive Branch?

Good point. Probably not. Federal prosecutors have broad discretion over whether to bring charges or not, and it's unlikely they'll do so against an executive branch official, especially if the person being held in contempt is the attorney general, the nation's top law enforcement official.

Also, the president has called subpoenas the "weapon of choice" for Democrats' "all-out political war" and vowed to fight them all, especially those related to his family's finances or business dealings.

Have We Been in this Situation Before?

Yes, and there is precedent. Most recently, US attorneys cited their prosecutorial discretion to justify decisions not to pursue contempt charges against former White House Counsel Harriet Miers and then-White House Chief of Staff Joshua Bolten in 2008, and Atty. Gen. Eric H. Holder Jr. in 2012. Then, like now, the executive branch was under one party while the House was controlled by the other.

Is There Anything Else Congress Can Do?

Yes, it can go to federal court. That's the next option, but it's a time-consuming one. Either the House or Senate can file a lawsuit in federal district court seeking a declaration that the person is legally obligated to comply with the congressional subpoena.

But Trump would likely try to delay turning over any information to the House until after the 2020 election. It took four years after Holder was held in contempt for the courts to rule that the Obama administration had to hand over documents Republicans had requested about detailing the botched Fast and Furious gun sales operation.

If the court rules in Congress' favor, the person can be held in contempt of court and jailed.

Any Other Options?

Yes, but it's rare these days and controversial, relying on a congressional authority known as "inherent contempt." That method hasn't been used since 1935.

Inherent contempt was once a fairly common tactic used by Congress to ensure compliance. This route involves a person being arrested by the sergeant at arms of the House or Senate, and brought before the full House or Senate for a trial. In this case, it would effectively involve the House ordering the arrest of the nation's attorney general. That's no small step.

The person is then tried by the chamber that brought the contempt charge. If convicted, the person is imprisoned—possibly on the Capitol grounds—until they agree to comply. They would be released when Congress decides or when the two-year congressional session ends.

What About Impeachment?

That's another possibility. Democrats so far have been reluctant to impeach Trump, but they might be less hesitant to impeach an unelected official such as Barr.

The problem is that even if the House votes to impeach, that is only the first part of the proceeding. Because impeachment involves both chambers, it is the Senate, now under Republican control, that would have the power to convict—which requires a two-thirds vote—and remove a person from office. That was the situation when the House voted to impeach President Clinton and the Senate refused to convict him.

Impeachment is the biggest weapon in Democrats' arsenal, but it is extreme and could backfire if voters perceive it to be politically motivated.

EVALUATING THE AUTHOR'S ARGUMENTS:

Viewpoint author Sarah D. Wire explains the challenges Congress faces when trying to impeach someone from the executive branch or hold them in contempt. Does this seem to be reasonable, in order to keep one branch of government from getting too powerful? Or do the problems caused outweigh that benefit?

Chapter 2

What Are the Controversies over Executive Privilege?

Opinions about executive privilege often depend on the party represented in office.

Leave the President Alone

"The president is subject to the rule of law, but the dignity and demands of his office afford him protections unavailable to others."

Craig Trainor

In the following viewpoint, Craig Trainor defends President Trump's use of executive privilege in attempting to prevent administration officials and advisers from testifying before Congress. The author implies that the Democrats were investigating Trump in order to take down a political opponent. The author argues that the president does, in fact, have more rights than other politicians or the average citizen. Craig Trainor is a criminal defense and civil rights attorney.

AS YOU READ, CONSIDER THE FOLLOWING QUESTIONS:
1. Why does Congress have the power to investigate the president?
2. How can Congress abuse its power to investigate the president?
3. In the author's view, why is the president more important than an individual member of Congress?

"Executive Privilege Is Fundamental," by Craig Trainor, Manhattan Institute for Policy Research, Inc., September 12, 2019. Reprinted by permission from City Journal.

The House Judiciary Committee, led by Democratic congressman Jerry Nadler, is moving steadily toward initiating impeachment proceedings against President Trump. The president's repeated assertion of executive privilege in his legal conflict with Nadler is the latest example of his alleged disregard for the rule of law. Nadler previously subpoenaed former White House counsel Don McGahn and former White House communications director Hope Hicks. Corey Lewandowski, Trump's first campaign manager, along with Rick Dearborn and Rob Porter—both former White House aides—were also recently summoned to testify. They join a long line of targeted administration officials, including Jeff Sessions, Rod Rosenstein, John Kelly, and Jared Kushner. Undoubtedly, Trump will assert executive privilege to prevent his administration officials and advisors from testifying before the congressman's committee, as he did with McGahn and Hicks—and the media will find lawyers to claim these assertions are overbroad, baseless, and dangerous.

What's lost in these talking points is definition, context, and rationale. As a threshold matter, executive privilege is neither novel nor sinister. Its historic pedigree was established by George Washington, who, in 1792, reserved the right to withhold from Congress the content of White House deliberations and records that it sought regarding the death of 600 US soldiers in a Native American ambush along Ohio's frontier. Washington asserted it again, in 1796, when he refused to disclose to the House of Representatives documents related to the Jay Treaty, which sought to resolve outstanding issues with Great Britain. Washington's example reminds us that executive privilege is not some obscure legal theory manufactured by Richard Nixon to conceal his duplicity in connection with Watergate.

In discharging his responsibilities, the president must receive candid, and often unpopular, advice from his advisors. In *United States v. Nixon*, the seminal case on executive privilege, the Supreme Court reasoned that "the importance of this confidentiality is too plain to require further discussion. Human experience teaches that those who expect public dissemination of their remarks may well temper candor with a concern for appearances and for their own interests to the detriment of the decision-making process." The specter of public

George Washington set the precedent for the US presidency. While he was very clear about limiting the power of the position, Washington did in fact invoke executive privilege.

disclosure would chill open deliberation among the president's men and, as a result, impede energetic executive action.

For Congress or the courts to compel disclosure of these discussions would allow co-equal branches of government to infringe on the unique role that the president plays in the American constitutional order. Unlike congressmen, senators, and judges, the president alone is vested with executive power. Though the Constitution is silent on the matter, the Supreme Court reasoned that "the privilege can be said to derive from the supremacy of each branch within its own assigned area of constitutional duties. Certain powers and privileges flow from the nature of enumerated powers; the protection of the confidentiality of Presidential communications has similar constitutional underpinnings."

Executive privilege has limits. Like the executive, Congress has "its own assigned area of constitutional duties." Under its Article I legislative power, Congress holds the authority to investigate and conduct oversight of the executive branch and compel the production of testimony and documents to this end. Congress's implied power to investigate emanates from its express power to legislate. As the Supreme Court put it in *McGrain v. Daugherty*, in 1927: "The power of inquiry—with process to enforce it—is an essential and appropriate auxiliary to the legislative function."

This authority enables Nadler's committee to issue subpoenas for Trump's cabinet officials and advisers. And if one is on the business end of a congressional subpoena, one does well to take it seriously. Failure to comply may result in a visit from the House of Representatives' Sergeant at Arms—a man empowered to arrest and imprison contumacious witnesses unless and until they comply with the subpoena. Alternatively, Congress can cite the disobedient witness for contempt and refer the matter to the United States

FAST FACT

In *United States v. Nixon*, the Supreme Court noted that "those who expect public dissemination of their remarks may well temper candor with a concern for appearances ... to the detriment of the decision-making process."

Attorney's Office for the District of Columbia for criminal prosecution. Finally, Congress can request a court order commanding the subpoenaed target to comply.

The validity of executive privilege claims is rarely litigated because the threat of constitutional crisis hangs over any assertion of power by one branch over another. Politics is thus the primary method of adjudicating these competing claims—and politics favors the popular. The American president, however, should not be hampered in executing his critical functions just because he's out of favor with the MSNBC crowd.

The solution, as it were, is a call to statesmanship—or appealing to the better angels of Nadler's nature and, to a lesser extent, Trump's. If Nadler can resist the temptation to investigate Trump, in the words of Earl Warren, "solely for the personal aggrandizement of the investigator or to punish those investigated," then he has a patriotic opportunity to transcend petty partisanship. "Through the normal political process of confrontation, compromise, and accommodation," as one expert on executive privilege explained, Congress and the president can "resolve their differences over executive privilege" disputes. We will not cease hostilities in the misguided partisan constitutional warfare of the last two decades by "resorting to the solution that was rejected by the Framers—that is, by demanding constitutional certitude."

The Supreme Court has made clear that executive privilege commands that Congress and the courts bear a "very heavy responsibility to see to it that Presidential conversations . . . are accorded that high degree of respect due the President of the United States." The president is subject to the rule of law, but the dignity and demands of his office afford him protections unavailable to others. John Marshall alluded to this status at the trial of Aaron Burr for treason, writing that "in no case of this kind would a court be required to proceed against the president as against an ordinary individual."

Executive privilege, however, is not designed to serve the president's personal interests, but those of the public. It recognizes the presidency's unitary and unique constitutional commitments. *Federalist 70*, written by Alexander Hamilton, explains "energy in the Executive is a leading character in the definition of good government. It is essential to the protection of the community against foreign attacks . . . to the steady administration of the laws . . . [and] to the security of liberty against the enterprises and assaults of ambition, of faction, and of anarchy." There is only one chief executive.

Nadler, on the other hand, for all his pontificating on Trump's "richly deserved" impeachment and his condemnation of the president's claims of executive privilege, is one of many. The Constitution does not charge him with defending the nation, prosecuting foreign wars, receiving and acting on intelligence briefings, or appointing Supreme Court justices. He should execute his oversight responsibilities with the dignity, humility, and seriousness befitting his office. After all, he is easily replaceable in his next election. I ought to know—I'm one of his constituents.

EVALUATING THE AUTHOR'S ARGUMENTS:

Viewpoint author Craig Trainor argues that executive privilege is designed to serve the interests of the public. At the same time, he claims that the president has additional responsibilities that give him additional freedoms. Do you think the president should be held to different standards from other people? Why or why not? Does executive privilege serve the common good, the president's personal interests, or both?

Viewpoint 2

"The attorney-client privilege does not exist between Congress and the executive branch because they have the same client—the American people."

Executive Privilege Can't Shield Wrongdoing

Todd F. Gaziano

In the following viewpoint, Todd F. Gaziano argues that executive privilege should not be invoked to shield misdeeds. The author cites the case of Operation Fast and Furious, a gun-running investigation during the Obama administration. He contends that the administration's invocation of executive privilege to avoid releasing subpoenaed documents is a clear violation of executive power. Todd Gaziano is Pacific Legal Foundation's chief of legal policy and strategic research.

"Executive Privilege Can't Shield Wrongdoing," by Todd F. Gaziano, The Heritage Foundation, June 22, 2012. Reprinted by permission.

AS YOU READ, CONSIDER THE FOLLOWING QUESTIONS:

1. What is the "Fast and Furious debacle" referenced in the viewpoint?
2. What pertinent point did the Supreme Court make in *United States vs. Nixon*?
3. What bright spot resulted from Attorney General Eric Holder's request of President Obama, according to the author?

As a strong defender of executive power (when properly exercised) and executive privilege (when properly invoked), I am concerned when claims of executive power or privilege are abused for any reason—especially if they are invoked to shield potential wrongdoing. In addition to shielding the wrongdoing, it jeopardizes the very executive power that the president is entrusted with when Congress and the courts react—as they did in the post-Watergate era—to the abuse of power.

The House Committee on Oversight and Government Reform is rightfully investigating the Fast and Furious debacle, in which the administration allowed thousands of guns to flow across the Mexican border, resulting in the death of one US border patrol agent and at least 200 Mexican citizens, according to the Mexican attorney general. The most glaring violation of executive power in that investigation before now was the refusal of the Department of Justice (DOJ) to turn over 1,300 pages of documents subpoenaed by the committee without even an assertion of executive privilege. Attorney General Eric Holder simply refused on his own initiative in a blatant act of stonewalling.

As Holder surely knew all these past months, there is no privilege that exists between Congress and the executive branch to withhold documents except the constitutional executive privilege, which is based on the separation of powers. For example, the attorney-client privilege does not exist between Congress and the executive branch because they have the same client—the American people. Holder also knew that executive privilege does not attach to documents automatically. It can be asserted only by the president or with his direct approval. It can be waived; indeed it should be waived in many or

When Attorney General Eric Holder was held in contempt of Congress in 2012, it was the first time Congress had taken such a dramatic move against a sitting cabinet official.

most instances when Congress needs the information for its legislative functions. So the slated House committee vote to hold Holder in contempt on Wednesday was unfortunately necessary to get him to at least reconsider his lawless course of stonewalling.

In a desperate attempt to prevent the contempt vote in the last few hours, Holder asked President Obama to invoke executive privilege to shield these 1,300 pages of documents from Congress, and the president agreed to do so. Yet that is not the end of the story. Even if properly involved, the Supreme Court has made clear that executive privilege is not absolute. DOJ must provide an explanation why all those documents fit one of the recognized categories of executive privilege. It is questionable whether they all are legitimately subject to executive privilege, for several reasons.

First, the Supreme Court in *United States v. Nixon* (1974) held that executive privilege cannot be invoked at all if the purpose is to shield wrongdoing. The courts held that Nixon's purported invocation of executive privilege was illegitimate, in part, for that reason. There is reason to suspect that this might be the case in the Fast and Furious cover-up and stonewalling effort. Congress needs to get to the bottom of that question to prevent an illegal invocation of executive privilege and further abuses of power. That will require an index of the withheld documents and an explanation of why each of them is covered by executive privilege—and more.

Second, even the "deliberative process" species of executive privilege, which is reasonably broad, does not shield the ultimate decisions from congressional inquiry. Congress is entitled to at least some documents and other information that indicate who the ultimate decision maker was for this disastrous program and why these decisions were made. That information is among the most important documents that are being withheld.

Third, the Supreme Court in the Nixon case also held that even a proper invocation must yield to other branches' need for information in some cases. So even a proper invocation of executive privilege regarding particular documents is not final.

And lastly, the president is required when invoking executive privilege to try to accommodate the other branches' legitimate information needs in some other way. For example, it does not harm executive power for the president to selectively waive executive privilege in most instances, even if it hurts him politically by exposing a terrible policy failure or wrongdoing among his staff. The history of executive-congressional relations is filled with accommodations and waivers of privilege. In contrast to voluntary waivers of privilege, Watergate demonstrates that wrongful invocations of privilege can seriously damage the office of the presidency when Congress and the courts impose new constraints on the president's discretion or power (some rightful and some not).

But there is at least one helpful development in Holder's request that the president invoke executive privilege to shield these documents: The president now owns the consequences of further stonewalling. There is no ongoing DOJ prosecution or investigation to protect. There is no obvious reason why the president can't waive even what legitimately privileged documents there are (which is probably far fewer than the 1,300 pages being withheld).

The American people will now clearly understand that it is President Obama who doesn't want them to know who is to blame for the Fast and Furious scandal—and whether his administration has done anything to prevent it from happening again.

EVALUATING THE AUTHOR'S ARGUMENTS:

Viewpoint author Todd F. Gaziano opens his viewpoint by stating his stance on executive power and executive privilege. Do the specifics of the situation he takes issue with support that stance?

We Don't Always Have a Right to Know

Michael Schudson

"It is not difficult to think of instances where reasonable people would prefer that some information the government possesses be kept from the public."

In the following viewpoint, Michael Schudson argues that secrecy in government was accepted until the 1970s, when higher education became more common in the US and students and professors challenged authority. The author believes that many changes toward a more transparent government are good, yet privacy also has its benefits. He considers cases where government secrecy is legal and valuable, referring to the case of Edward Snowden, a subcontractor for the National Security Agency (NSA), who collected secret documents showing that the US government was spying on citizens. Michael Schudson is a professor of journalism at Columbia University.

AS YOU READ, CONSIDER THE FOLLOWING QUESTIONS:
1. What are some examples of when government information should be kept secret from the public?
2. When did a record of politicians' votes become available to the general public?
3. What led to the Freedom of Information Act?

"The Right to Know versus the Need for Secrecy: The American Experience," by Michael Schudson, ABC Religion & Ethics, May 5, 2015. Reprinted by permission.

Thomas Jefferson once wrote that "information is the currency of democracy," or so it is easy to learn online. Fortunately, it is just as easy to learn that he wrote no such thing. The people who run the website for Jefferson's home at Monticello cannot find that quotation anywhere in Jefferson's papers.

And there is really no need to spend time searching. The American founders rarely spoke of democracy and they did not label the American form of government "democratic" but "republican." They judged democracy to be unstable and undesirable. So we can feel confident that Jefferson never uttered nor wrote these words.

It was not Jefferson but political activist Ralph Nader who declared information the currency of democracy. In 1970, Nader claimed a "well-informed citizenry" to be the "lifeblood of democracy," and wrote that "information is the currency of power." Later, in 1986 and 1996, he condensed these not entirely consistent propositions into: "Information is the currency of democracy."

Nader's proposition, however, stands on shaky grounds. It is not difficult to think of instances where reasonable people would prefer that some information the government possesses be kept from the public.

In the interest of public safety, a citizen who is being watched by undercover police officers, operating according to the law, should not be informed of the surveillance. In the interest of personal privacy, the public should not have access to personnel records of government employees without good cause. Nor should genuine national security information be publicly available.

Activists who support transparency in government do not generally advocate complete transparency in all facets of government. Most democrats accept many limitations to complete disclosure of government information.

In the United States, many of these limitations are long established and well institutionalised, including their incorporation in explicit provisions of the pioneering United States Freedom of Information Act (FOIA) of 1966. This was the first such law in the world since Sweden enacted something like it in 1766 and Finland in 1951.

Earlier in North American history, there were many conditions under which subjects—later "citizens"—did not have full access to

The Freedom of Information Act allows any person to request access to federal agency records unless the records are protected by exemptions or exclusions contained in the law.

relevant information. It troubled the government of Virginia in 1682 that an upstart printed the laws of the colony without a licence. He was punished, since printing was forbidden in Virginia until 1729, and from that point until 1765 the governor controlled the only printing press in Virginia.

In the Commonwealth of Massachusetts, a political entity with an elected assembly, legislative proceedings were confidential, even including how one's representative voted on particular measures. It is hard to imagine a matter more central to democracy than the availability to voters of a public record of how their representatives vote, but this was not something the people of Massachusetts in the 1700s demanded.

Nor did the people of the United States demand it until 1970–1970! Only then did the US House of Representatives make members' votes on amendments to bills part of the public record. Only then did a reform coalition in the House sponsor a set of "antisecrecy" measures that ushered in a major increase in the public visibility of legislative action.

What Can We Learn from History?

There are several important historiography lessons in all this.

First, there is a strong tendency, at least in the United States, to attribute all wise political acts and ideas to people who lived at the end of the eighteenth century and correspondingly to attribute all ill-conceived and disastrous political ideas to our contemporaries—particularly those of the other party. Yet when we look closer, this assessment of history requires re-adjustment, especially to account for the dramatic ways in which democracies have come to operate at least since 1945. While these changes are problematic in various respects, they also incorporate huge advances in pluralism, tolerance, diversity of representation and transparency.

Second, sources of progressive change do not always come "from below." In some instances they do—the US civil rights movement is a stunning example. (Although, even there, a long history of the NAACP's legal efforts to challenge segregation and discrimination operated in the courtrooms of the nation, not in the streets.) But in the particular case of the right to know, the drive for freedom of information was pursued with scarcely any popular interest, let alone a popular movement.

The Freedom of Information Act came out of a decade-long effort in the Congress to control the expansion of an ever more powerful executive branch of government. This was much more a battle between two branches of government than between two political parties or two theories of governing. It appealed to a popular Cold War rhetoric, urging members of Congress to recognise that growing executive power and executive secrecy were establishing a "paper curtain" in Washington, violating principles of "openness" that distinguished the "free world" from Soviet totalitarianism.

Presidents both Republican and Democrat resisted the congressional challenge; members of Congress both Republican and Democrat vigorously urged it forward. While journalists and associations of journalists like the American Society of Newspaper Editors applauded FOIA, the general public took little notice.

Third, there is a challenge that few scholars have taken up concerning the role of higher education itself in fostering both insight and oversight as public values. Higher education in the United States grew enormously after 1945 in the percentage of young people attending college. Even more important, it changed decisively in the development among college faculty and students of a more critical attitude toward received cultural knowledge. This included a growing integration of the sciences into college curricula once largely dominated by the arts and letters. Over time, as historian Thomas Bender has observed, "The increasingly professionalised disciplines were embarrassed by moralism and sentiment; they were openly or implicitly drawn to the model of science as a vision of professional maturity."

Tracing the impact of higher education on the broader society is a task that deserves far more attention than it has received. One of those impacts, I suspect, was a growing resonance of challenges to authority, including the authority of public officials who operate behind closed doors.

Sometimes There Are Good Reasons for Secrecy

Making government more accessible to the public is vital to improving the quality of democracy, yet this does not make transparency an ultimate good that should be honoured under all circumstances. There really are military secrets that should not fall into the hands of fanatics, practical jokers, or deranged people. There really is a need for government decision-makers to be able to trust in the confidentiality of their meetings and of their electronic communications if there is to be a free flow of conversation among them.

The recent dust-up over Hillary Clinton's use of her personal email account while in office as US Secretary of State is only the latest case of uncertainty over the rules of acceptable behaviour when there is a clash between a legitimate confidentiality of internal communications and a public right to information. Should the Secretary of State be forbidden to shield some of her communications by conducting them on her personal email account?

What about a professor at a public university? Should he or she be able to shield communications in the same fashion, making them unavailable to citizens who use state public records laws to demand release of emails? Some groups have sought access to professors' email to discredit researchers whose work supports the scientific consensus on climate change. Others have tried to discredit professors who are sceptical of the scientific consensus. Some states exempt university professors' records from public records laws on the grounds that the preservation of academic freedom is a vital democratic good that, within limits, trumps the public's right to know.

There really are good reasons for, say, the secrecy of the voter's ballot in a world where the strong can intimidate the weak if their preferences are known. There really are good grounds for protecting privacy and, in the realm of everyday social interaction, maintaining civility by tact in the withholding of honest appraisals. And there really is a value in authentic intellectual inquiry related to public issues that deserves to be weighed against a public right to know.

Still, reforms toward the greater visibility of government activity and demands for greater frankness in other domains of life, too, have contributed to the improvement of society. Almost everyone recognises the danger to democracy of overclassification and enforced silences that exist only to save an individual, office or policy from embarrassment and not to protect national security, personal privacy or decision-makers' legitimately confidential deliberations.

So What About Edward Snowden?

And Edward Snowden? Snowden has indicated that he has not released all of the government records in his possession. Nor, apparently, will he do so. Some of them, it seems, if made public, could endanger public safety.

I have no reason to doubt Snowden's good intentions in withholding these records, but nor do I have any reason to judge him an expert at, let alone a legitimately selected representative for, deciding what information is or is not in the public interest. Why is this his right to decide?

Responsible government secrecy requires a democratic process of oversight. Theft, brave and selfless an act as Snowden's appears to have been, is not a good model of holding government accountable.

I understand the distrust of government secrecy. I share it. I do not understand a lack of distrust of informational vigilantism and even, in some quarters, antic glee at Snowden's coup. We can be grateful that he opened a window on wide-ranging US government misdeeds in National Security Agency surveillance, but it is much harder to sympathise with the way he went about it.

In a world of grave dangers to life from weapons we have made, of devastating threats to earth's resources that we have callously exploited, and of hate and intolerance we have failed to sanction, it is often difficult to see bright spots in recent decades, but surely one of them is an expansion of a culture of frankness and of expectations of public disclosure.

These advances are not untroubled, as anyone who honours the value of privacy knows, but on balance there has indeed been progress.

EVALUATING THE AUTHOR'S ARGUMENTS:

In this viewpoint, author Michael Schudson argues that there should be a balance between privacy and secrecy. How can people determine where that line should be? Do you believe the current situation is acceptable, or should it change in one direction or the other?

Executive Privilege Ends with Impeachment

"Impeachment provides the defense against permanent destruction of the Republic."

David M. Driesen

In the following viewpoint, David M. Driesen explores the use of executive privilege during an attempt at impeaching a president. In the author's view, presidents should not be able to use executive privilege to avoid sharing information during an impeachment trial. Driesen notes that a president's advisers should be encouraging the president to follow the law. He believes this will be more likely if the advisers know they might have to testify about the advice they gave. Therefore, the author suggests, executive privilege should end when impeachment begins. David M. Driesen is a professor at Syracuse University College of Law. The American Constitution Society for Law and Policy is a progressive legal organization.

"Executive Privilege and Impeachment," by David M. Driesen, American Constitution Society, October 3, 2019. Reprinted by permission.

1. Does executive privilege apply when a president is under investigation in a criminal case?
2. How does impeachment differ from a criminal case?
3. In the author's view, how would removing executive privilege from impeachment cases encourage the president to follow the law?

Mike Pompeo has signaled that he plans to invoke executive privilege to avoid disclosure of statements or documents relevant to impeachment. This will raise a crucial constitutional issue—whether executive privilege can be invoked to hinder an impeachment proceeding. There is a strong case that executive privilege should not limit disclosures to relevant House Committees in the impeachment context.

The Supreme Court has never held that executive privilege applies in the impeachment context. Instead, it created the privilege in the context of a dispute about discovery of communications between President Nixon and White House advisors in a criminal case not aimed at Nixon himself, but at his advisors and campaign staff. Nixon was only an unindicted co-conspirator in that case. Because of the case's context, the Court focused on balancing the President's confidentiality interests against the judicial system's need to reach a just verdict in a criminal case.

In the context of a criminal case, it held that the privilege cannot trump the need to disclose information essential to reaching a just verdict. If executive privilege applied in the impeachment context it could not block disclosure of information essential to the impeachment inquiry. The Supreme Court rejected the notion that executive privilege is an absolute privilege in *United States v. Nixon*. The case for allowing the executive branch to withhold essential information is even weaker in the impeachment context than in the criminal trial context. Executive privilege cannot prevent disclosure of information essential to resolving the inquiry into whether the House should impeach the President and the Senate should remove him from office.

It follows that the executive branch cannot refuse to disclose information demanded by congressional entities investigating or carrying out impeachment or removal. Rather, Congress would have to judge whether information it received should be disclosed to the public in light of the considerations that animate executive privilege in the criminal context. Several principles support this conclusion.

First, impeachment is, in part, a political process. Congress must make an informed political judgment about whether the President's conduct betrays the public trust in such a serious way as to make him unfit to remain in office. Informed political judgment requires that executive branch officials must disclose any information arguably relevant to such an inquiry. Because impeachment necessarily requires value choices by politicians with varying views about what betrayal of the public choice is, the essentiality decision cannot partake of the neat logic possible when a single judge makes a ruling about violation of a carefully defined offense under the criminal code. There must be broad latitude in making the essentiality judgment.

The second principle relevant to whether executive privilege should exist in this context involves the need to give proper weight to the impeachment process itself. The *Nixon* Court required disclosure of matters essential to resolution of a criminal case, because of the weighty due process concerns at issue in deciding whether to convict officials accused of crimes. Making sure that the impeachment process is fully informed is an even more weighty consideration. Impeachment is intended as a remedy to prevent a reversion to despotism. The Framers put impeachment in the Constitution to make sure that the rule of law survived, not just for a few individuals, but for all Americans. It safeguards the entire democratic system upon which liberty depends.

The third principle stems from the rarity of impeachment, which has only occurred twice before in our history (not counting the Nixon resignation). Allowing disclosure of all information even arguably relevant to an impeachment inquiry would not generally impair the executive branch's operation. The *Nixon* Court based executive privilege on the need to protect candid communication between the President and his advisors. But Presidents rarely engage in conduct that necessitates impeachment, so a rule of full disclosure in the face of impeachment will not limit candid advice in the overwhelming majority of cases. Although criminal conduct by the President and his aides is not common either, it is much more common than presidential bribery, treason, or high crimes and misdemeanors. And most of those advising a President so unfit for public office as to potentially merit impeachment will likely offer candid advice even if disclosure might ensue, as they would want to counsel him to stay within the law. Furthermore, we want to discourage advisors from encouraging Presidents to violate their oath of office. Impeachment with no executive privilege would reinforce officials' obedience to their constitutionally required oath of office, which demands that they swear obedience not to the President, but to the Constitution. In other words, we want to discourage candid advice about how best to evade the law or serve a foreign power to which a corrupt President is beholden (something mentioned by the Framers as a central concern).

The rarity and importance of impeachment should generally outweigh even the need to protect information vital to national security. The *Nixon* Court suggested that information damaging to our national security provides a stronger case for confidentiality than other kinds of material. But the Framers established impeachment, in part, to prevent a President beholden to a foreign power from remaining in office. In other words, it was designed to protect our national security from a disloyal President, even one who commits treason. Therefore, the need for the material necessary to resolve an impeachment inquiry must take priority over other information that might in some way temporarily damage our national security. Impeachment provides the defense against permanent destruction of the Republic, the very quintessence of what national security is all about.

Impeachment is an important tool in maintaining checks and balances.

The President cannot withhold information based on executive privilege even if he wishes to assert that the privilege applies. Initiation of an impeachment inquiry suggests that many elected representatives believe that the President may not be trustworthy. The inquiry exists to address problems like self-dealing and betrayal. A President meriting impeachment is very likely to abuse executive privilege or to interpret it generously in his favor. Furthermore, since impeachment is the remedy for treason, the procedures governing it must permit quick action when necessary, unobstructed by a self-interested President. Therefore, the President should turn over all information requested by relevant House committees, while noting which information it thinks should not be publicly disclosed and why. If the President resists, the courts should promptly order full disclosure to the relevant House committees, but not necessarily the public.

The question then arises about whether the House committees get to decide questions of whether it should keep information the President regards as privileged, confidential, or instead, the courts should resolve them. *Nixon* held that the courts should decide questions of privilege when the President asserts the privilege as a defense to discovery in a criminal case. It is not obvious that the courts should adjudicate presidential claims that the House should keep information it finds pertinent to its impeachment inquiry confidential, which necessarily arise outside of an ongoing court proceeding.

Separation of powers principles, practicality, and precedent counsel against the courts intervening to limit public disclosure of information in an impeachment proceeding. The Supreme Court has held that the Constitution commits questions of how to conduct an impeachment to Congress and that questions relevant to how Congress proceeds are therefore non-justiciable political questions. That principle would imply that the Constitution itself commits the issue of how much relevant information to disclose to the public to Congress when it commences an impeachment proceeding. Information, after all, is the center of a rational impeachment decision. If the Supreme Court ends up with an executive privilege issue, it should not undertake a balancing of the information needs of Congress against that of the President. It should simply hold that executive privilege does not apply in this context, but suggest that the Congress should consider the impact of public disclosure on national security and appropriate candid advice (which it will be inclined to do anyway).

More broadly, Mike Pompeo mentioned separation of powers concerns with information disclosure. While it is common to speak of separation of powers and checks and balances in one breath, in fact, they are in tension. The Constitution does not completely separate powers. It requires checks that breach the wall between branches. Impeachment, of course, constitutes the ultimate check and balance. It empowers Congress to remove any official of the other branches of government for betraying the public trust. Like all checks, it stands as an exception to the rule of rigidly separated powers. And honoring this check especially is crucial to the Constitution's survival.

Impeachment's importance as a check on a dangerous President suggests that executive privilege cannot apply once an impeachment proceeding begins. Allowing it to apply constitutes an unconstitutional interference with the congressional authority to determine how to process impeachments.

Executive Privilege Is Not Absolute

"Once executive privilege is asserted, the co-equal branches of the government are set on a collision course."

Alan Shapiro

In the following viewpoint, Alan Shapiro explores cases where executive privilege was considered by the courts. One involved nine US attorneys who were appointed by George W. Bush and then fired by the Department of Justice in 2006. After this piece was written, the DC District Court rejected the position that presidential aides had absolute immunity. The judge noted that executive privilege might allow an aide to refuse to answer specific questions, but it did not allow them to refuse to give testimony before a congressional committee. Alan Shapiro is an educator and cofounder of Morningside Center for Teaching Social Responsibility.

AS YOU READ, CONSIDER THE FOLLOWING QUESTIONS:

1. What was the Watergate scandal?
2. How did Watergate affect the legal understanding of executive privilege?
3. Why did President Bush invoke executive privilege in 2007?

"Presidential Power: Executive Privilege," by Alan Shapiro, Morningside Center for Teaching Social Responsibility, October 24, 2007. Reprinted by permission. https://www.morningsidecenter.org/teachable-moment

When George Washington was president, he refused a request by the House of Representatives for documents about the Jay Treaty with England. His reason was that the Constitution gives only the Senate, not the House, a role in ratifying treaties. This was the beginning of what has become known as "executive privilege."

The Constitution says nothing about this privilege, which has never been clearly defined. But since Washington, it has been invoked by presidents and mostly accepted by the other two branches of the government.

Congress did not accept it in 1974, though, when a struggle over executive privilege erupted. At the time, the big news in the United States was the Watergate scandal. It involved a criminal break-in of Democratic National Committee headquarters at the Watergate office and apartment complex two years earlier that possibly involved President Richard Nixon and his associates. Congress was investigating the administration's possible illegal use of government agencies and illegal wiretapping of newspaper reporters, among other things. Congress demanded audiotape recordings of private discussions between President Nixon and his closest advisors that might shed light on their investigation.

Claiming executive privilege, President Nixon refused. The deadlock resulted in the first formal recognition of executive privilege by the Supreme Court. It ruled that:

1. The Constitution gives the president a privilege to deny disclosures of his private conversations with close advisors.
2. But the privilege is not absolute and can be overcome when the "weight of legitimate competing interests" are involved. In this case, the Court decided that the need for evidence in a criminal trial was enough to deny that privilege.

The tapes implicated the president in criminal activities. When it became clear to President Nixon that he would be impeached and convicted, he resigned, the only president ever to do so.

Soon after President Bush took office in 2001, a controversy developed over Vice President Dick Cheney's refusal to supply information to Congress about the energy executives he met with when developing the Bush administration's energy policy.

The issue eventually came before the Supreme Court. The administration argued before the court that supplying Congress with the information it requested would be an "unwarranted intrusion" and "extreme interference" with the president's exercise of his "core" constitutional responsibilities. "Congress does not have the power to inhibit, confine or control the process through which the president formulates the legislative measures he proposes or the administrative actions he orders," the administration's brief argued.

The president's claim of executive privilege was upheld in 2004 by the Supreme Court. But Justice Anthony Kennedy warned, "Once executive privilege is asserted, the co-equal branches of the government are set on a collision course."

Another collision course began in December 2006 when the Department of Justice fired nine US attorneys. President Bush had appointed all of them after he took office in 2001, and they had been approved by the Senate, along with dozens of others. The White House said that the president had not been involved in the firings.

The US has a total of 93 attorneys, who are in charge of federal prosecutions. Traditionally, an incoming president asks for resignations of all the attorneys and appoints new ones from his political party. The attorneys serve at the pleasure of the president. But it is unusual to request resignations and make new appointments, as in this case, during a presidential administration.

Democrats, in the majority of both houses of Congress after the 2006 elections, began asking questions. Congressional committees called the dismissed attorneys to testify. The attorneys testified that they had not been fired because they were incompetent, but rather for political reasons.

For instance, former US attorney Paul Charleton of Arizona said he was fired for investigating Congressman Rick Renzi, an Arizona Republican, for his involvement in a crooked land deal. Daniel Bogden

EXECUTIVE PRIVILEGE

IMPOUNDING OF FUNDS

VETO POWER

CONGRESS

Ed Valtman '73　The Hartford Times

'DON'T PUT UP ANY RESISTANCE! JUST KEEP IN STEP'

Executive privilege can be a slippery slope. Once it is invoked, it forces the branches to collide.

of Nevada was fired while in the midst of overseeing an FBI investigation into the alleged bribing of Nevada's Republican governor, Jim Gibbons, by a military contractor while Gibbons was in Congress. Carol Lam of California said she was terminated for following the bribery trail that began with former Republican House member—and current prison inmate—Randy "Duke" Cunningham (www.citizen.org). US attorneys are supposed to be impartial in their investigations and to uphold the law regardless of the party they belong to.

The judiciary committees in the House and Senate, headed by Democrats, wanted testimony and e-mail records from such Bush administration advisors as Harriet Miers, former White House counsel, and Joshua Bolton, the chief of staff. Although President Bush had stated earlier that he had not been involved in discussions or actions related to the fired attorneys, Bush now claimed executive privilege, refusing to allow his aides to appear before the committees. The administration argued, "The assertion of executive privilege here is intended to protect a fundamental interest of the presidency: the necessity that a president receive candid advice from his advisers and that those advisers be able to communicate freely and openly with the president."

However, the president did offer to allow his aides to meet informally and privately with committees so long as they were not under oath and no written records were kept of what they said. The lawmakers refused.

On July 26, 2007, the House Judiciary Committee voted 22-17 along party lines to hold Miers and Bolton in contempt of Congress. Committee chairman John Conyers Jr., a Michigan Democrat, said the action was necessary "not only to gain an accurate picture of the facts surrounding the US attorneys controversy, but to protect our constitutional prerogatives as a coequal branch of government." The committee rejected the White House's claim of executive privilege.

This conflict between Congress and President Bush has not been resolved.

EVALUATING THE AUTHOR'S ARGUMENTS:

Viewpoint author Alan Shapiro considers how previous executive privilege cases were received by Congress and the Supreme Court. Do these cases suggest how current and future challenges should be resolved? Where would you draw the line in what executive privilege is allowed to keep secret?

Chapter 3

What Is the Future of Executive Privilege?

The future of executive privilege depends on how future presidents test it.

Viewpoint

1

The Past Doesn't Tell Us the Future

Richard Lempert

"It appears that neither the executive nor the legislative branch wants to cede power to the third branch, the judicial, to decide."

In the following viewpoint, Richard Lempert argues that when presidential aides make immunity claims, the courts rarely decide whether those claims are valid. When cases do go to the courts, the findings may only apply in certain narrow cases. This makes it difficult to say definitely when executive privilege does and does not apply. That means each president may test the law in new ways, and the future may bring different legal opinions to executive privilege. Richard Lempert is Professor Emeritus of Law and Sociology at the University of Michigan.

AS YOU READ, CONSIDER THE FOLLOWING QUESTIONS:
1. What is meant by the term "elbow aides"?
2. Which branch of government gets to decide the scope and conditions of executive privilege?
3. Are there differences between the protections given to written and spoken advice to the president?

"All the President's Privileges," by Richard Lempert, The Brookings Institution, December 19, 2019. Reprinted by permission.

President Trump has limited the information the House has had available for its impeachment and other investigations, by repeatedly instructing both current and past members of his administration to refuse to recognize the authority of congressional subpoenas. The president's claim is that executive privilege immunizes his close aides from an obligation to testify before or to turn over to Congress documents in their possession. Trump's exercise of this claim to withhold evidence from Congress forms the basis for the House's second article of impeachment. If President Trump is correct and his aides and their records are immune from subpoena, then he will have acted within his sphere of executive authority, and Impeachment Article II, for obstruction of Congress, is likely to fail. However, as applied to anyone other than the president himself, this is an extreme and questionable interpretation of the protections executive privilege affords, as evidenced by Judge Ketanji Brown Jackson's decision in November. In it she rejected former White House counsel Don McGahn's claim that executive privilege immunized him from having to appear before the House Judiciary Committee in response to its subpoena.

Claiming immunity for top aides is not, however, unique to this president—although he has pushed the envelope beyond what his predecessors have argued. Since Nixon, both Democratic and Republican presidents have made executive staff immunity claims. Seldom, however, have these disputes played out to the end; it appears that neither the executive nor the legislative branch wants to cede power to the third branch, the judicial, to decide. Instead, immunity claims usually result in negotiations between Congress and the executive, ending either with the surrender of one side (often after the situation triggering the standoff is no longer politically fraught), or with a negotiated compromise in which the committee issuing the subpoena typically gets some but not all of the information the executive originally tried to withhold.

There is little law that is directly on point. Before the McGahn case, only one of the few cases that passed on the legality of broadly claimed executive privilege involved an individual's refusal to appear before a Congressional committee. In this case, a House committee sought testimony from Harriet Miers, President Bush's White

House counsel, regarding the replacement of seven US attorneys, allegedly let go for unsavory political reasons. D.C. District Court Judge John Bates rejected Miers' claim of immunity, holding that she was required to appear and give testimony, although Bates did note that executive privilege might support refusals to respond to particular questions. Judge Jackson largely endorsed the reasoning of Judge Bates in justifying her decision. The Miers case did not, however, settle the law, even for the District of Columbia (the district in which her case was heard). Although Judge Bates' opinion is detailed and thoughtful, it was never reviewed on the merits by a higher court because the appellate process was unlikely to be finished before the expiration of the 110th Congress, at which point the committee's subpoena would lapse. Other than *Miers* and *McGahn* the few other cases dealing with executive branch claims to immunity all deal with subpoenaed documents.[1]

As Judge Jackson noted in her opinion, legal arguments for allowing a president's aides to claim immunity from Congressional subpoenas are mainly found in Department of Justice (DOJ) memoranda, usually prepared by the Office of Legal Counsel (OLC), and mainly citing arguments in earlier OLC memoranda as justification. These DOJ opinions are not case law and read more like partisan briefs than dispassionate legal analyses.

The fount of later DOJ opinions is one rendered in 1971 by William Rehnquist, then head of OLC and later Chief Justice of the Supreme Court. Rehnquist advanced two main justifications for his opinion supporting immunity, neither of which holds up well to scrutiny. The first is that the president's top aides are on call 24/7 and that if they were busy testifying before Congress they might be unavailable when the president needed them. This claim made little sense when first advanced and makes even less sense today when electronics allows virtual meetings at a moment's notice. The second argument, more favored in later justifications, was that a small number of highest-level advisors ("elbow aides") are the president's alter egos and share the president's (assumed) separation-of-powers-based immunity from Congressional subpoenas. This argument, however, appears untenable following Supreme Court decisions in the companion cases of *Nixon v. Fitzgerald* and *Harlow v. Fitzgerald*.

The George W. Bush administration's assertion of executive privilege to prevent White House counsel Harriet Miers from testifying before Congress was rejected by the DC District Court.

These cases involved a civil suit by a whistleblower who claimed that Nixon and two top aides conspired to eliminate his job because he had disclosed to Congress substantial cost overruns in a military procurement program. Taken together, the cases hold that a (former) president may not be sued civilly for actions taken in his capacity as president, but aides who assisted him in any decision do not enjoy absolute immunity. In other words, even close presidential aides do not step into the president's shoes when claiming legal process immunity. The president's lawyers, however, seek to avoid the precedential force of *Harlow* by arguing that aides with different responsibilities than Harlow's are not necessarily covered by this precedent. A fair reading of *Harlow* does not support this argument, but a court that wanted to find for Trump could distinguish *Harlow* on these grounds.

The few other cases in which presidents have sought to use executive privilege as an absolute shield against Congressional subpoenas involve documentary requests and so, unlike *Miers*, are not directly on point. Nevertheless, several principles appear clear. First, the scope and conditions of executive privilege are for the judicial branch to decide, notwithstanding the executive's status as a separate branch of the government. This was a core holding in *US v. Nixon*, and has been reiterated in later opinions. Second, separation of powers arguments are not irrelevant. Some measure of executive privilege is implied by the Constitution. Third, the president's status appears unique, and the full scope of the immunity that a president might claim is not shared by even his closest assistants. Fourth, the protections of executive privilege as they relate to subpoenas are, apart from the Congress's presumed inability to haul the president before it, not absolute. Rather they are subject to qualifications, which may include balancing the need for evidence against the values the privilege protects. Fifth, in deciding whether to honor a claim of executive privilege, a judge in some circumstances may review allegedly privileged material in chambers to decide if a privilege should attach.

Given these principles and earlier OLC arguments, it would appear that some of the immunity claims advanced by President Trump on behalf of his aides seek to stretch the law of executive privilege beyond its acknowledged boundaries. Indeed, in the case of some witnesses who have been instructed not to testify, the stretch is extreme. In particular, claiming immunity for staff who are not direct reports to the president, for members of the cabinet or their staff, and for people who have left the government would require the courts to go far beyond rethinking the availability of subpoena immunity for the closest active presidential aides.

But in a case as politically charged as the current ones and with a Supreme Court that is perhaps polarized politically and uncommonly willing to overturn precedent, today's law may not be the rule tomorrow. Moreover, even within the bounds of what has been decided, there is, without dramatically breaking from precedent, a narrow window for upholding the president's claims. A 1953 Supreme Court decision, *US v. Reynolds*, gave lower courts almost no discretion to deny claims of executive privilege when there is on its face a plausible case that the privilege has been invoked to protect military secrets, and it limited substantially the trial court's ability to review the allegedly privileged material in chambers to determine if that material in fact involved military secrets. Moreover, several more recent decisions denying executive branch personnel immunity from subpoenas suggest that a different analysis might have applied if military or foreign policy secrets were at issue. The suggestion reflects dicta in *US v. Nixon* leaving open the possibility that presidential communications might be immune from subpoena if a need to protect military, diplomatic, or sensitive national security secrets is claimed. A court that so desired could treat information relating to interactions with Ukrainian President Zelensky and his staff as diplomatic secrets intended for communication to the president whose details courts cannot probe, and it could hold that executive branch officials are immune from subpoena if called solely to testify on matters related to "negotiations" with Ukraine.

If the trial before the Senate takes the legal issues seriously, disputes over whether President Trump was privileged to order aides not to appear and to withhold from Congress subpoenaed documents are likely to be central to the disposition of the second impeachment count. If, as many expect, Republican senators vote against conviction despite apparent facts, they may justify their votes by saying that President Trump's assertion of immunity as an executive privilege was in accord with the law. Only a definitive Supreme Court decision, which if it comes at all will come long after the Senate trial, could prove the Senators wrong.

Whatever happens in the impeachment trial, the question of whether executive privilege allows a president's close aides to ignore subpoenas is not going to go away. *McGahn*, which is on appeal, arose long before the House began impeachment proceedings, and one can expect that future attempts by the House to investigate the president's actions will also generate subpoenas to officials who will make immunity claims even if impeachment is not in issue. If current precedent holds, the courts are likely to reject immunity claims made on behalf of or by executive branch officials, but this will not mean, as Judge Jackson took pains to point out in *McGahn*, that these officials will have to answer all the questions committee members ask.

Two widely accepted privileges may justify refusals to answer. These are the deliberative process privilege, which protects pre-decisional deliberations involving the president, cabinet secretaries, or other executive department officials, and the presidential communications privilege, which protects communications to and from the president, even if they are not part of an identifiable decision-making process.[2]

The deliberative process privilege is a common law privilege, while the presidential communications privilege is rooted in the separation of powers, making it the more protective of the two. Moreover, the "close aide" restriction that OLC opinions treat as applying to executive branch immunity claims is less likely to limit the scope of protected information when the presidential communications privilege is invoked. In the most thorough judicial treatment of this privilege, Judge Patricia Wald, writing in 1997 for a panel of the D.C. Circuit Court in *In re Sealed Case*, held that the presidential communications privilege protected documents produced by lower-level White House staff even if they were never communicated directly to the president, so long as they were part of a chain of information requested by top presidential staff for use in advising the president. Presumably the same principle would apply if the privilege were claimed to prevent lower level staff from testifying to information conveyed to superiors that would have been protected had it been embodied in documents. The deliberative process privilege might, however, be the only available privilege if discussions among subordinates were not in response to requests from top level presidential aides or related to polices that they had the authority to implement without higher level consultation.

The *In re Sealed Case* opinion states explicitly that the panel's analysis would not necessarily apply where subpoenaed documents were sought not for law enforcement purposes, as they were in that case, but by the Congress.[3] Nevertheless, it seems safe to draw certain conclusions from Judge Patricia Wald's careful analysis and from privilege law in general. First, presidential communications protected by the deliberative process privilege would also be protected by the presidential communications privilege, though the converse is not true. Thus, only the contours of the presidential communications privilege need be examined to determine what information executive branch officials cannot be required to disclose so long as the information was assembled at the direction of the president or a top executive office aide. Second, the privilege is a qualified privilege and not an absolute one. This means that if presumptively privileged evidence is not available from non-privileged sources, testimony or document production can be compelled if the need for the evidence is great enough. However, the need hurdle that must be overcome is a substantial one, not easily surmounted. Third, the presidential communications privilege applies only to communications relating to the president's official duties. If, for example, a top presidential aide told President Trump while he was sitting in the Oval Office that his hotels had lost money in 2018, the communication would not be protected. Fourth, where the privilege does apply, its protective umbrella is a broad one, covering communications that originate in the work of lower-level staffers and reach the president's ears, if they do at all, only through one or more staff intermediaries. If a president's direct report decides not to relay to the president information sought in order to better advise him, the communication nonetheless remains protected. In effect, it is the potential utility of the communication in advising the president and not its actual use that matters in evaluating the privilege.

The limits of the presidential communications privilege are likely to have much in common with the limits on other confidential communications privileges, perhaps with a special bow to its Constitutional roots. For starters, communication privileges do not bar testimony to what a witness knows apart from the communication, except to the extent that the contents of a protected communication might be directly inferred from such testimony. Suppose, for example, that a staffer listening in on the July 25 call to Ukrainian President Zelensky noticed that even though Joe and Hunter Biden's names were mentioned in the call, the transcript of the conversation did not mention them. If the staffer called a superior's attention to the omission, the privilege might allow or even require the staffer to refrain from responding when asked by a House member if he had reported the omission to a superior. The assumption would be that the report was eventually intended for the president. The member could, however, ask the witness if he had noticed any discrepancies between what he

FAST FACT

The judges considering *In re Sealed Case* (also known as the Espy ruling) decided that "communications made by presidential advisers in the course of preparing advice for the President come under the presidential communications privilege."

had heard and the transcript of the call. The presidential communications privilege would not apply because the witness would be asked about what he personally knew and not about what he had told his superior.

Communications privileges are also typically waivable by the privilege holder. Presidents can waive their communications privilege, and most often they do. Hard problems can, however, arise when waivers are not explicit. For example, the release of part of a privileged document, or testimony to part of a privileged conversation, is frequently held to waive the privilege with respect to withheld portions of the document or conversation, even if a full waiver was not intended. Imposed waiver is particularly likely if the portrait painted by the released information would change significantly if all the privileged information were revealed. The privilege, it is said, serves as a shield and not a sword. Indeed, courts go further. The voluntary release of otherwise privileged information or documents can be held to waive the privilege as to any otherwise privileged documents that deal with the subject matter of the disclosed document. Thus, President Trump's statements regarding what some people told him about events transpiring in Ukraine could be held to waive the privilege as to all communications prepared for or received by him with respect to these events. But the presidential communications privilege's roots in the Constitutional system of separated powers means it is unlikely to be treated like other communications privileges in this respect. Rather, courts are likely to refuse to treat partial disclosures, even if done for strategic reasons, as waiving the privilege with respect to undisclosed related material.

Privileges are also held to be waived, or may not attach in the first instance, if the circumstances surrounding a communication or later disclosures by the privilege holder of what was said suggest that confidentiality was not a serious privilege holder concern. For example, if Ambassador Sondland had told President Trump at the outset of his July 26 cell phone call from a Kyiv restaurant that he was calling over an insecure line and that people nearby might overhear the conversation, by any conventional analysis no privilege would attach to the conversation. However, a court might treat a claimed presidential communications privilege differently, arguing perhaps that a presidential judgment about whether a conversation was so urgent that it had to proceed despite the danger of being overheard had to be respected. Similarly, disclosing privileged information in non-privileged relationships or contexts (telling a golfing buddy for example, what one told the attorney general) typically vitiates other confidential communications privileges, but a court might be unwilling to second guess a president's judgment about whom to confide in or where.

Communication privileges also do not protect otherwise privileged disclosures when the disclosures were made for the purpose of perpetrating a crime or fraud. In *In re Sealed Case* mentioned above, Judge Wald succinctly summarizes the D.C. Circuit Court's view of the state of the law as it applies to the executive privileges. The deliberative process privilege "disappears altogether when there is any reason to believe governmental misconduct occurred." The presidential communications privilege is somewhat more protective, for the party seeking to overcome the privilege "seemingly must always provide a focused demonstration of need, even when there are allegations of misconduct by high-level officials."

The communications privilege that is perhaps most familiar to the public is the attorney-client privilege and its associated attorney work product protections, which almost anyone who consults a lawyer can claim. If current law holds, President Trump may have difficulties in claiming the attorney-client privilege to prevent testimony on matters relating to Ukraine. Not only is the attorney-client privilege subject to the communications privilege exceptions described above, but it may not apply in the first instance. A federal circuit court decision, which the Supreme Court declined to review, held that the president is not the White House counsel's client for purposes of the privilege. Rather the White House counsel's client is the government. However, this case is not directly on point, for it addressed claims that arose out of a grand jury and not a legislative subpoena. The same is true of the few other cases addressing the issue, one of which allowed the privilege to be claimed, albeit by the Connecticut governor and not by the president. As for Rudy Giuliani, should he be called to testify, the fact that he is the president's personal attorney should not matter with respect to much of what he might be asked about. The privilege only protects communications with attorneys for the purpose of securing legal services. Giuliani's activities in relation to Ukraine may be serving the president, but they appear not to be legal services. Moreover, even if they were, he could most likely be compelled to testify to actions he has taken unless they were such that they would reveal confidential communications from Trump to him. And there is an additional wrinkle. Although the Congress usually respects the attorney-client privilege, except where the Constitution requires otherwise, it can set its own rules of procedure. It might demand that communications that would be privileged in a court of law be disclosed, although for political reasons, if not for reasons of principle, it is unlikely to do so.

Finally, there is a non-communication privilege for state secrets, which the Supreme Court recognized in the *Reynolds* case mentioned above, and which has since figured in other cases. It is an unusual privilege in that the privilege is not held by the witnesses or parties in a case, but the government can step in and exclude evidence by claiming the privilege even if the competing litigants do not object to its admission. The privilege if claimed by the government is, however, of uncertain application in the context of Congressional hearings, though rules regarding classified information may affect what information can be disclosed in public or heard by whom. Moreover, *Reynolds* concerned itself only with military secrets, and although subsequent attempts by Congress to codify a state secrets privilege have included in the protected category foreign policy relevant information along with military information, the most prominent efforts have applied only to the introduction of such evidence in civil litigation and have allowed for various levels of in camera review to determine whether governmental efforts to invoke the privilege are justified. Hence the Trump administration is unlikely to succeed in preventing Ukraine-related testimony by invoking this privilege. If, however, questions regarding its applicability were taken to court, the resulting delay might be an effective bar to ever hearing what the executive sought to exclude.

Applying existing law as it is best understood today would mean that the immunity claims that Trump has advanced to prevent aides from testifying will not avail him, and that his ability to benefit from the various communication privileges is likely to be fact dependent and perhaps of limited value. This is true without considering a unique feature of the House's most recent subpoenas: that they were issued in connection with an impeachment investigation. Had the House chosen to pursue the legal enforcement of these subpoenas or if contempt charges against some who refused to testify are ever adjudicated, this could matter. To the extent that Trump's claim that Congress cannot subpoena his aides to testify has a leg to stand on, that leg is grounded in the Executive's constitutional status as a coequal branch of government. But there is one respect in which the Constitution does not treat the president as coequal with the Congress. This is with respect to impeachment. The Congress is given the power to remove the president, but the president enjoys no similar power over Congress or its members. If claims of executive privilege are viewed with this in mind, the separation of powers argument for a broad reading of executive privilege is less persuasive in an impeachment hearing setting than in any other context where Congress demands of the executive information.

My summary and conclusions reflect existing law. The future is not, however, necessarily predictable from the past, and even if precedent is mainly respected, there are few relevant and no controlling Supreme Court decisions on the precise issue that President Trump's immunity claims raise. Hence the Court, with its conservative majority, could veer from the path that the law of executive privilege has taken and uphold the claims of immunity that have been advanced to protect the president. I think, however, that this is unlikely, even if one of the justices who would hear the case is the son of Anne Gorsuch who, as EPA administrator, was the first person Congress ever held in contempt for refusing to turn over subpoenaed documents in compliance with a presidential order to claim immunity.

What is more likely is that President Trump will prevail in a game that has been played by his predecessors with some success. This is to snatch victory from the jaws of probable defeat by using the delays built into judicial processes to forestall a controlling decision until information sought is no longer politically useful or subpoenas have lapsed with the seating of a new Congress. Thus, D.C District Court Judge Ketanji Brown Jackson's late November ruling—that Donald McGahn must testify despite the claim that he is immune from Congressional subpoena—although not stayed beyond seven days by Judge Jackson, has been temporarily stayed by the D.C. Circuit Court until January 3, when it will hear a motion not on the merits but with respect to a further stay pending appeal. Unless a further stay is denied, which seems unlikely, or the appeal process is rapidly expedited, it will be some months before a circuit court decision is handed down. If that decision goes against McGahn, a further appeal to the Supreme Court, with an accompanying stay, is almost certain, and a decision by the High Court before the end of its current term is not guaranteed. Thus, without ever breaking the law or resisting a final court ruling, McGahn is likely to be able to keep what he knows to himself until long after what he could disclose could have figured in impeachment proceedings and perhaps even past the 2020 election.

Notes

1. Another case raising, on slightly different facts, the issues resolved by the district courts in *Miers* and *McGahn* is a declaratory judgment action brought by former Trump national security aide Charles Kupperman, joined by John Bolton. The action ostensibly seeks guidance on whether it is the Congressional subpoena to testify or the presidential order not to appear before Congress which must be obeyed. It appears likely that this case will be dismissed on standing or mootness grounds because the House has withdrawn the subpoenas directed at Kupperman and Bolton and said that it will not reissue them. Moreover, the president and the House, each of which are responding parties, agree that the case should be dismissed, citing a number of different grounds, including standing, mootness, ripeness and immunity from suit. The House's stated reason for withdrawing its subpoena, which it did a week after Kupperman filed his case, is that pursuing the litigation would unduly delay its proceedings, as it certainly would have if its Intelligence Committee felt that it had to await a final judicial resolution of the matter before concluding its impeachment investigation. It is possible, however, that an additional and maybe a truer reason was that the case had been assigned to Richard Leon, a senior judge and one of the most politically conservative judges on the D.C. District Court. Had Judge Leon held that the president's executive power allowed him to preclude his aides from testifying, this would have undermined, if not destroyed, the impeachment resolution's "Obstruction of Congress" count, even if the judge's ruling was

later overturned on appeal. (In theory Congress could claim that a president's invocation of a valid privilege to prevent testimony before a House committee obstructed the Congress, but the claim would almost certainly be politically untenable.)

2. The existence of these privileges has been used to counter some of the otherwise strongest arguments made on behalf of a presidential right to claim immunity for close advisors since they mean that if a president's close aides must appear to testify they will nonetheless be able to avoid testifying about their communications with the president. Thus, arguments that without immunity there will be a chilling effect such that a president and his close advisors will feel unable to converse frankly appear overblown. Moreover, neither of these privileges are absolute. If there may be circumstances where even advice given directly to the president is unprotected by privilege, it is difficult to make the case for an absolute privilege not to appear.

3. *In Re Sealed Case*, 116 F3rd 550, grew out of a grand jury inquiry into the actions of President Clinton's Secretary of Agriculture, Mike Espy, who was alleged to have improperly accepted gifts from entities affected by Agriculture Department actions and policies. President Clinton had earlier ordered White House counsel to look into the Espy matter, and the Office of Independent Counsel (OIC), which had convened the grand jury, sought to secure documents related to the White House investigation. Clinton claimed executive privilege with respect to some of these documents, and the district court, after in camera review, denied OIC's document request in its entirety. OIC appealed, and the D.C. Circuit Court held that the district judge had to reconsider some of its earlier judgments. What makes the case important is Judge Wald's exceptionally thoughtful and thorough discussion of the precedents affecting the existence and scope of the presidential communications privilege and her enunciation of standards to apply in deciding whether claims of privilege should be honored. It is unclear whether Judge Wald's exclusion of congressional subpoenas from the ambit of her opinion is meant to suggest that claims of executive privilege are weaker or more robust when a subpoena has been issued by Congress, so it is best interpreted as meaning only that when Congress has issued the subpoena additional issues are raised that the panel has not addressed.

EVALUATING THE AUTHOR'S ARGUMENTS:

In this viewpoint, author Richard Lempert considers the complicated law surrounding executive privilege. Because the courts can take so long to resolve a challenge, many presidential aides delay answering questions for months or years. Is it important to let the courts decide these cases, no matter how long it takes? Are there other ways the situation could be handled?

Look to History to Understand the Limits of Executive Privilege

Katrina Mulligan and Aminata Diallo

"The executive privilege does not protect the president when he is acting in his personal capacity."

In the following viewpoint, Katrina Mulligan and Aminata Diallo explore the impeachment trial against President Donald Trump in more detail. The White House tried to keep current and former employees from testifying or tried to limit what they could say. Some employees testified anyway. These authors describe situations where executive privilege would and would not apply in legal cases. Katrina Mulligan is the managing director for national security and international policy at the Center for American Progress. Aminata Diallo was an intern for national security and international policy at the Center for American Progress.

"The Executive Privilege Is Far from Absolute," by Katrina Mulligan and Aminata Diallo, Center for American Progress, October 16, 2019. Reprinted by permission.

AS YOU READ, CONSIDER THE FOLLOWING QUESTIONS:
1. Why is it important to separate the president's official duties from his personal concerns when considering executive privilege claims?
2. Does executive privilege allow presidents to keep their decisions or actions secret?
3. Does executive privilege provide immunity to congressional subpoenas?

For a man who says he has nothing to hide, President Donald Trump and his administration seem to want to keep an awful lot hidden. Following a week of depositions and testimony featuring acting Director of National Intelligence Joseph Maguire and the US Intelligence Community Inspector General Michael Atkinson, the White House abruptly changed course last week, signaling a shift in its approach to the impeachment inquiry. On October 8, after the State Department reportedly ordered US Ambassador to the European Union Gordon Sondland not to appear for a deposition with House investigators, the president's chief legal adviser informed House leadership that President Trump and his administration would not comply with the impeachment inquiry. Subpoenas immediately followed.

Remarkably, despite White House efforts to block her participation, former US Ambassador to Ukraine Marie Yovanovitch decided to appear before House investigators—and she may have inspired others to step forward, too. Fiona Hill, former White House adviser on Russia, appeared before House investigators on Monday, and Ambassador Sondland is expected to appear before House investigators on Thursday, despite earlier White House efforts to keep him quiet. Although the White House continues to try to limit what current and former administration employees can say, lawyers representing those employees have pushed back, arguing that the executive privilege does not apply. With a number of hearings and document production deadlines looming, there will be many opportunities for the White House to attempt to withhold cooperation.

Presidents may invoke executive privilege in order to ensure confidential and effective counsel from their advisers.

The White House's central claim is that it is not required to turn over certain documents or to permit certain testimony because the information pertains to deliberations that are protected from disclosure under the executive privilege, a long-standing doctrine rooted in the separation of powers that permits the executive branch to protect the confidentiality of presidential deliberations. The US Supreme Court has recognized the president's constitutionally based privilege to withhold certain information from disclosure to the public or Congress—but these constraints are far from absolute. There are important limitations on the president's ability to withhold information from Congress.

What the Executive Privilege Does— and Does Not—Protect

The executive privilege exists to protect the president's legitimate interest in, at least under some circumstances, preserving the confidentiality of internal communications that is essential to effective consultation. Presidential claims of a right to protect the confidentiality of information from disclosure to Congress have been a common theme in executive-congressional relations dating back to the late 1700s. Since then, presidents have withheld information from Congress when its disclosure would harm national security or impede sensitive negotiations as well as for the purpose of ensuring they receive effective counsel from their advisers. As former President Dwight D. Eisenhower said in 1955:

> *There is no business that could be run if there would be exposed every single thought that an adviser might have, because in the process of reaching an agreed position, there are many, many conflicting opinions to be brought together. And if any commander is going to get the free, unprejudiced opinions of his subordinates, he had better protect what they have to say to him on a confidential basis.*

However, the executive privilege is not absolute, and it is important to be clear about what the executive privilege does not protect.

The executive privilege does not protect the president when he is acting in his personal capacity.

The privilege only protects deliberations that relate to the president's official duties. It therefore does not protect communications that relate to personal matters such as an incumbent president's or his advisers' communications related to political campaign work.

The executive privilege does not protect information related to presidential decisions once they have been made.

The privilege is intended to protect deliberations and permit the flow of confidential ideas—not to conceal the president's decisions or the actions that flow from them. Therefore, if communications relate to a decision the president has made or direct federal employees to undertake activities on the president's behalf, the executive privilege does not apply.

The executive privilege does not protect communications related to the current or future commission of a crime.

To the extent that the communications relate to a potential violation of law, they would not be protected from disclosure under the privilege.

The executive privilege does not protect communications that are never received by the president or his office.

Communications between the president's agents—such as text messages between parties that do not include the president or White House officials—are not protected by the privilege.

The executive privilege cannot provide absolute immunity to congressional subpoenas.

Courts have found that Article I of the US Constitution grants Congress the "power of inquiry," and this power carries with it the "process to enforce it." Subpoenas issued pursuant to an authorized investigation are therefore, as one court put it, "an indispensable ingredient of lawmaking." And history supports this: Since the 1970s, more than 70 senior advisers to the president who were subject to subpoenas have testified before congressional committees.

As the impeachment inquiry continues, the limitations on the executive privilege and the president's ability to protect communications from disclosure to Congress are sure to come into greater focus. As that happens, impeachment watchers should scrutinize claims of executive privilege because, while the executive privilege has an important place in the separation of powers, history and the judicial record show that it is far from absolute.

EVALUATING THE AUTHORS' ARGUMENTS:

In this viewpoint, authors Katrina Mulligan and Aminata Diallo argue that executive privilege has many limits. Does this sound like the authors' opinion, or do they provide enough evidence to support these claims?

Viewpoint 3

Executive Privilege Can Be Taken Too Far

"If the legislative branch is to enforce the rule of law, witnesses must be compelled to answer legitimate questions under oath."

Chris Edelson

In the following viewpoint, Chris Edelson argues that President Trump tried to place himself beyond the rule of law. His aides refused to testify because, they said, the president might want to claim executive privilege later. However, executive privilege should only be claimed in specific cases with a legal basis. The author notes that Congress can put additional pressure on a president but might be unlikely to do so when politicians are from the same party as the president. Chris Edelson is assistant professor of government at American University School of Public Affairs.

AS YOU READ, CONSIDER THE FOLLOWING QUESTIONS:
1. What was the problem with Attorney General Jeff Sessions's refusal to answer questions before the Senate Intelligence Committee, according to the author?
2. What can a president do to delay or stop an investigation?
3. What can Congress do to put pressure on a president who is keeping aides from testifying?

Donald Trump's presidency has been defined by a central theme: Trump's belief that ordinary rules and laws do not apply to him.

Trump has made clear that he believes it is up to his personal discretion to order torture—even though torture is illegal under all circumstances. In ordering a military strike against Syria in April, Trump brushed aside constitutional requirements that Congress approve such action unless the US faces imminent attack. And he has defended his presidency by falsely claiming that the president is incapable of having conflicts of interest.

I have argued in the past that Presidents George W. Bush and Barack Obama showed there is reason to be concerned about post-9/11 presidents testing the legal limits of their power. The stakes are even higher now with Trump. He has demonstrated authoritarian tendencies and contempt for the rule of law that goes beyond anything Bush or Obama did.

The issue may be coming to a head with investigations into Russian interference in the 2016 election and possible obstruction of justice. As the nation has watched witnesses appear before congressional committees and read Trump's tweets about Department of Justice officials, the key question to ask now is whether Trump will refuse to let any investigation continue. If he does so successfully, Trump will effectively place himself beyond the reach of the law.

The Rule of Law

The various ongoing investigations are all, in theory, governed by legal rules. Special Counsel Robert Mueller's task is to speak to witnesses, review documents, gather evidence and decide whether there is any basis for prosecution under federal law. Congressional committees, meanwhile, hear from witnesses who testify under penalty of perjury if they lie under oath.

But such legal rules are not self-enforcing. When the rules are violated or flouted, someone has to act in order to give them force and meaning.

Attorney General Jeff Sessions' recent testimony before the Senate Intelligence Committee is a case in point. Sessions refused to answer a number of questions about communications he'd had with the president. By itself, that is not extraordinary. If the communications were protected by executive privilege or involved classified information involving national security matters, there may have been a legitimate basis for Sessions to decline to answer senators' questions. After all, the Supreme Court has recognized that the Constitution implicitly allows the president to invoke executive privilege in some circumstances in order to protect the confidentiality of discussions with close advisers in the executive branch.

But Sessions, the top lawyer for the US government, did not point to any legal grounds for his refusal to respond. He simply said he could not speak about private conversations he'd had with the president, and that he was protecting Trump's ability to claim executive privilege, if he later decided to do so.

Sessions was not the first. A week earlier, Director of National Intelligence Dan Coats similarly declined to answer questions involving conversations he'd had with the president. Like Sessions, Coats did not invoke privilege, conceding that he wasn't sure there was any legal basis he could rely on.

As Sen. Martin Heinrich noted during the hearing, that's not the way executive privilege is supposed to work. If the administration wants to invoke the privilege, it must do so expressly. In that case, the matter would be worked out either in negotiations between the executive and legislative branches or (less frequently) through review by the federal courts.

The most famous example of a court weighing in on executive privilege was the Supreme Court's 1974 decision in *US v. Nixon*. President Richard Nixon's administration refused to hand over Oval Office tapes, claiming recorded conversations were protected by executive privilege, as defined by the president. The court rejected this view, observing that constitutional separation of powers depends on checks and

Fast Fact

On May 17, 2017, Robert S. Mueller III was appointed as special counsel to look into links between Russia and the Trump campaign, the Russian government's efforts to interfere in the 2016 election, and related matters.

The position of the US presidency is not meant to enjoy unchecked power.

balances that prevent any one branch from self-policing. The court found, in this case, the need for checks on power outweighed the executive branch's interest in keeping discussions confidential. With the specter of impeachment looming over him, Nixon was forced to hand over the tapes. He resigned from office a few weeks later.

At the close of Sessions' testimony, Sen. Richard Burr instructed Sessions to "work with the White House to see if there are any areas of questions that they feel comfortable with you answering…" That's not good enough: If the legislative branch is to enforce the rule of law, witnesses must be compelled to answer legitimate questions under oath.

Will Congress Act?

Special Counsel Mueller may be investigating the president to determine whether his actions amount to an obstruction of justice. Trump has already fired former FBI Director James Comey, and there is speculation that he might also fire Special Counsel Mueller in an effort to bring the investigation to a close. Sen. Ron Wyden has warned that, if Trump fires Mueller, it would be an attack on the rule of law itself. The onus would fall squarely on Congress to either initiate impeachment proceedings or else acquiesce in a presidential power grab.

As Sen. Heinrich noted, when witnesses refuse to answer questions but fail to provide any sufficient legal reason for doing so, they are obstructing investigation—preventing Congress from carrying out its inquiry. If other senators agreed, they could vote to cite the witness(es) for contempt, which could lead to criminal prosecution.

Congress could also threaten to hold up Trump's nominations to key positions such as federal court judges, or refuse to move on the administration's legislative priorities like tax cuts for high earners (it took some similar actions in response to Nixon). Congress could even begin impeachment proceedings if it decided presidential misconduct rose to the constitutional level of "high crimes and misdemeanors"—for instance, if Mueller's investigation concluded that there is evidence to support this conclusion.

Of course, since Republicans are members of the same party as the president, none of this is likely—yet. But if Trump administration officials continue to make investigation difficult, and if Trump escalates an already tense situation by continuing to question Mueller's legitimacy or even by firing the special counsel, Republicans may face a crucial test on behalf of American constitutional democracy.

EVALUATING THE AUTHOR'S ARGUMENTS:

In this viewpoint, author Chris Edelson argues that President Trump tried to take executive privilege too far and obstructed justice. Do you agree with this conclusion? Why or why not? Did the author's strong opinion influence you?

The President Can't Override Laws

"A criminal justice apparatus cowed by the chief executive and wielded only according to his unchecked whims is the first step on the road to autocracy."

Frank Bowman

In the following viewpoint, Frank Bowman considers whether President Donald Trump had the power to fire special counsel Robert Mueller, who was investigating him. Some scholars supported the idea that Trump could fire Mueller on any grounds he chose. This author disagrees, arguing that the president is responsible for upholding all laws, including those that protect employees. Therefore, Trump could only fire Mueller with just cause. Frank Bowman is professor of law at the University of Missouri School of Law.

"The 'Take Care Clause' Does Not Permit Trump to Fire Robert Mueller Directly," by Frank Bowman, Impeachable Offenses, April 16, 2018. Reprinted by permission.

AS YOU READ, CONSIDER THE FOLLOWING QUESTIONS:
1. What is a regulation, in legal terms?
2. What is the "take care" clause?
3. What are two ways the take care clause might be interpreted?

In last Friday's *New York Times*, John Yoo and Sakrishna Prakash contend that President Trump has the power to fire special counsel Robert Mueller "directly," meaning without complying with the Department of Justice regulation mandating that a special counsel can be fired "only by the personal action of the Attorney General" (or if the AG is recused, his designee) and then only for "good cause," such as "misconduct, dereliction of duty, incapacity, [or] conflict of interest." In plain terms, they are saying that the president can simply ignore the Justice Department's chain of command and its regulations and fire Mueller for any reason or, as they insist, "no reason at all."

It is important to understand how radical this argument is. Most of the commentary about how Mr. Trump could fire Mr. Mueller accepts the premise that Justice Department regulations specifying how and by whom a special counsel can be removed are laws, binding both officers of the Justice Department and the president himself. Hence, the endless discussions of whether Trump will embark on a "Saturday Night Massacre" round of firings in search of a senior Justice Department official willing to behead Mueller.

To non-lawyers, it might seem odd that an internal departmental rule called a "regulation" is treated as equivalent to a "law." But in our legal system, departmental regulations promulgated using procedures prescribed in the "Administrative Procedure Act" are "law." And they are every bit as binding on presidents or anyone else as a congressionally enacted statute or a decision of the Supreme Court. The Justice Department's regulations on the special counsel are precisely this kind of regulatory law.

Yoo and Prakash try to evade this elementary reality of modern American jurisprudence by referring to Article II, Section 3, of the Constitution, which requires a president to "take care that the laws be faithfully executed." They say this constitutional language means that

In his capacity as special counsel for the US Department of Justice, Robert Mueller investigated ties between the Trump campaign and the Russian government.

the president has absolute control over the federal law enforcement function and thus can direct that legal actions be terminated and federal law enforcement officers fired whenever it suits him. According to them, the "take care" clause means that a president cannot be bound by any regulation, or indeed any statute that Congress might pass, purporting to limit his power to dismiss subordinates in the executive branch.

They're wrong. Though they focus here on the narrow issue of the tenure of a special counsel, their position is merely a local manifestation of the "unitary executive" theory occasionally fashionable on the fringes of the intellectual far right. It remains a fringe view because, if accepted, it would strike a crippling blow to the rule of law in this country.

Consider its effect in the law enforcement setting. If the Take Care Clause effectively overrides Justice Department regulations on the special counsel, it also overrides all statutory and regulatory rules purporting to safeguard federal employees from arbitrary dismissal. In that case, the president may not only fire a prominent special appointee like Robert Mueller, without process and without cause,

FAST FACT

Article II, Section 3 of the US Constitution (the "take care" clause) reads, in part: "[The President] shall take Care that the Laws be faithfully executed, and shall Commission all the Officers of the United States."

but also every career prosecutor, FBI agent, analyst, and secretary who worked on a case that displeased the president.

A criminal justice apparatus cowed by the chief executive and wielded only according to his unchecked whims is the first step on the road to autocracy.

Moreover, the extremist view propounded by Yoo and Prakash resonates far beyond criminal justice. After all, the president's obligation to ensure faithful execution of "the laws" is not limited to criminal statutes. It extends to all of the myriad laws—constitutional, statutory, and regulatory—that govern all aspects of our national existence. A president is every bit as obliged to ensure faithful execution of laws governing revenue collection, fair housing, collective bargaining, workplace safety, environmental protection, and the distribution of Medicare and Social Security benefits as he is to ensure proper administration of laws against fraud and official corruption.

Thus, if Yoo and Prakash are right, the president cannot constitutionally be prevented from firing any executive branch employee in any department whenever he feels that such an employee isn't executing the law as the president would prefer it executed. For them, legal protections against arbitrary or politically motivated dismissal can be of no effect so long as it is the president who orders a firing. In short, their reading of the constitution would effectively destroy the federal civil service system which, since 1883, has protected the country from the corruption endemic whenever a president or ruling party has unchecked power to dismiss federal employees who will not obey directions from political superiors.

No court will, or should, accept a reading of the constitution so contrary to long-settled legal norms and so destructive of the professionalism and political neutrality of federal civil servants.

It has been reported that the White House has sought advice on whether Robert Mueller might be directly dismissed, and that it has received some scholarly support for the idea. One hopes that Mr. Trump has not relied on ideas like those of Professors Yoo and Prakash, which combine the defects of being constitutionally unsound, unlikely to find acceptance in the courts, and deeply subversive of the rule of law.

EVALUATING THE AUTHOR'S ARGUMENTS:

Viewpoint author Frank Bowman is a law professor. Does that add weight to his argument? Why or why not? How might a thorough understanding of the law help or hinder debates about executive privilege and a president's actions? Compared with other viewpoints in this resource, how effective is this author's case?

Who Will Hold Power in the US Government?

Barbara L. McQuade

"The impeachment trial itself could cause all three branches to collide."

In the following viewpoint, Barbara L. McQuade raises questions about how President Trump's first impeachment trial might affect US government in the future. The courts usually avoid cases where branches of the government are in conflict. Instead, the opposing branches are encouraged to negotiate and compromise. However, Trump's impeachment trial pressured the courts to intervene in the conflict between the executive and legislative branches. This raised questions about how the executive, legislative, and judicial branches might act and interact in the future. Barbara L. McQuade is a professor at the University of Michigan.

The legal and constitutional battles sparked by President Trump's behavior could affect how the US government works for generations, long after the impeachment trial is over.

After the last Senate staffer turns out the lights, major questions remain to be decided outside of the Capitol about the limits of presidential power, the willingness of courts to decide political questions and the ability of Congress to exercise effective oversight and hold a president accountable.

Here are three of those questions.

What Are the Limits of Presidential Power?

First, the aggressive exercise of executive power by Trump has put this power under court scrutiny.

Trump's vow to "fight all the subpoenas" breaks from the traditional process—negotiation and accommodation—that previous presidents have used to resolve disputes between branches of the government.

As a result, several cases are currently pending, including a legal challenge brought by the House Judiciary Committee to compel the testimony of Don McGahn, Trump's former White House counsel. The House had sought McGahn's testimony about Trump's alleged obstruction of justice in the investigation of special counsel Robert Mueller into Russian election interference.

McGahn challenged the subpoena issued by the Judiciary Committee on the grounds of absolute immunity, arguing that he—a close aide to the president, and a member of the co-equal executive branch—need not appear before Congress to answer questions at all.

US District Judge Ketanji Brown Jackson rejected this argument, saying that while McGahn could possibly assert executive privilege about individual questions, he could not refuse to appear altogether.

Executive privilege is not specified in the Constitution. But the Supreme Court has recognized that a president may shield from disclosure certain sensitive information and communications to encourage candid advice from aides and to protect national security and other sensitive information.

"However busy or essential a presidential aide might be, and whatever their proximity to sensitive domestic and national-security projects, the President does not have the power to excuse him or her from taking an action that the law requires," Judge Jackson wrote.

The case is now on appeal, and during oral argument in early January, the committee's lawyer said that additional impeachment articles could be filed based on McGahn's testimony.

In 1974, in *United States v. Nixon*, however, the court stated that the privilege is not absolute, and must yield in some circumstances, such as a criminal investigation. Absolute immunity, which courts have not recognized, goes even further than executive privilege, permitting an aide to refuse to appear altogether.

Regardless of the outcome of the case, a court decision in the McGahn case will provide clarity that will weaken or strengthen the negotiating position of future presidents.

Should Courts Step into Political Conflicts?

Some of the cases still pending could determine how much power courts have in impeachment matters.

Under what is known as the "political question doctrine," courts typically avoid what are known as "political questions" that involve branches of government in conflict. They have dismissed most cases that present such questions, deferring to the other branches to resolve them. In the more than 200 years between 1789 and 2017, when Trump took office, courts heard only five cases for presidential claims of executive privilege in response to a congressional subpoena.

In the 1993 case of *Nixon v. United States* (no, not that Nixon, US District Judge Walter Nixon), the Supreme Court held that a federal judge could not appeal to a court seeking to overturn his conviction

Executive privilege is not specified in the US Constitution.

at a Senate impeachment trial. The Constitution, the court ruled, gives the Senate the sole power to try all impeachments.

Concurring opinions in the *Nixon* case, however, left open the possibility of an appeal to courts for an impeachment trial that was conducted "arbitrarily," that is, lacking procedural fairness.

Trump's personal lawyer, Rudolph Giuliani, suggested at one time that Trump file a court challenge to dismiss the articles of impeachment.

While that seems unlikely in light of the *Nixon* case, the political question doctrine is likely to figure in other pending cases, such the effort by Congress to seek grand jury material from Mueller's investigation.

During oral argument earlier this month in the case over grand jury material pending before the court of appeals, one of the judges expressed reluctance to decide the case because it involves a political question.

As the courts decide the cases involving McGahn's testimony, the Mueller grand jury material, and any challenge arising from Trump's impeachment trial, the contours of the political question doctrine will become more defined.

Will the Executive, Legislative and Judicial Branches Collide?

In the impeachment's aftermath, the extent of Congress' ability to serve as a valid check on presidential power will become more clear.

The framers of the Constitution envisioned a Congress that would provide oversight over a president. They did not count on members of Congress having more loyalty to their party than to their institution.

If the Senate were to acquit the president in the face of additional incriminating evidence, the institution's ability to serve as a credible check on future presidents could be damaged.

The impeachment trial itself could cause all three branches to collide. Former national security adviser John Bolton has publicly stated that he would testify if subpoenaed by the Senate. Trump has said he would invoke executive privilege to block Bolton's testimony.

If the Senate wanted to compel the testimony, the presiding Chief Justice John Roberts would decide the standoff between the president and the Senate. If he were to rule in favor of the Senate and order Bolton to testify, could President Trump appeal that decision to the Supreme Court? Would the Court be willing to decide such a political question about impeachment? Would the Senate arrest and jail a witness for refusing to testify?

There are no rules for what happens then.

Throughout his presidency, Trump has been a disrupter of normal procedures. It appears that he will continue that trend even after impeachment.

EVALUATING THE AUTHOR'S ARGUMENTS:

In this viewpoint, author Barbara L. McQuade raises questions brought about by Trump's impeachment trial. How do you think these questions might be answered in the future? Is it best to get legal answers, or should the branches of government focus on negotiation and compromise?

Facts About Executive Privilege and the Powers of the Presidency

Editor's note: These facts can be used in reports to add credibility when making important points or claims.

What Is Executive Privilege?

The US federal government has three branches. They are the executive (the president and about 5 million workers), legislative (Senate and House of Representatives), and judicial (Supreme Court and lower courts).

Executive privilege refers to the right of the president, and possibly other top executive branch officials, to withhold information from Congress and the courts, and therefore the public. Executive privilege usually applies in certain narrow circumstances. The first is related to national security needs, such as the movements of troops in wartime and the steps the government takes to stop terrorism. The second involves protecting the privacy of White House discussions when it is in the public interest to do so.

When presidential aides make immunity claims, the courts rarely decide whether those claims are valid. Instead, Congress and the president negotiate, or the standoff continues until the information is no longer important, and then the issue is dropped. When cases do go to the courts, the findings may only apply in certain narrow cases. This makes it difficult to say definitely when executive privilege does and does not apply. That means each president may test the law in new ways, and the future may bring different legal opinions to executive privilege.

History of Executive Privilege

The term "executive privilege" is not in the US Constitution. However, it is considered an implied power based on Article II, which is meant to make sure one branch of government doesn't become too powerful. Executive privilege helps limit the power of the legislative branch (Congress) over the executive branch.

Article I of the US Constitution describes the powers given to Congress. It does not expressly authorize either house of Congress to investigate the president and demand testimony. However, the Constitution gives Congress legislative power, the power to make laws. The Court has historically agreed that Congress needs the "power of inquiry"—the power to conduct investigations—in order to uphold the laws.

Some experts consider the idea of executive privilege to date back to George Washington's time. In 1792, he argued against turning over documents relating to an unsuccessful military operation against Native Americans. The specific phrase "executive privilege" was not yet used.

President Dwight Eisenhower evoked executive privilege more than 40 times, ushering in the modern era of its use. In 1954, Senator Joseph McCarthy demanded that White House officials testify about suspected communists. Eisenhower responded that anyone who testified to Congress about what advice they gave him would not be working for him by nightfall.

Impeachment

Impeachment is a process by which a legislative body, such as Congress, levels charges against a government official, such as the president. The US Constitution states: "The President, Vice President and all civil Officers of the United States, shall be removed from Office on Impeachment for, and Conviction of, Treason, Bribery, or other high Crimes and Misdemeanors."

Impeachment does not immediately remove the official from their position. Rather, it is the statement of charges against the official. To impeach the president, the House of Representatives starts the proceedings. House committees investigate, write the articles of impeachment (the charges against the president), and vote on the charges. A majority vote of at least 218 out of 435 representatives must approve the articles of impeachment. The US Senate then holds a trial, or the Senate can vote to dismiss the charges without a trial. If a two-thirds majority, 67 out of 100 senators, vote for impeachment, then the president is convicted and removed from office.

Impeachment votes often break down along party lines, Republican versus Democrat. If the president's political party also has a majority in the House or Senate, the president is less likely to be removed from office.

Three presidents have been impeached in US history: Andrew Johnson in 1868, Bill Clinton in 1998, and Donald Trump in 2019. However, Johnson, Clinton, and Trump were not removed from office because the Senate did not convict them with two-thirds of the vote. President Richard M. Nixon resigned when facing impeachment. Thus, no US president has been removed from office by impeachment.

Organizations to Contact

The editors have compiled the following list of organizations concerned with the issues debated in this book. The descriptions are derived from materials provided by the organizations. All have publications or information available for interested readers. The list was compiled on the date of publication of the present volume; the information provided here may change. Be aware that many organizations take several weeks or longer to respond to inquiries, so allow as much time as possible for the receipt of requested materials.

American Civil Liberties Union (ACLU)
125 Broad Street, 18th Floor
New York NY 10004
(212) 549-2500
contact form: www.aclu.org/general-feedback
website: www.aclu.org
The ACLU is a nonprofit organization founded "to defend and preserve the individual rights and liberties guaranteed to every person in this country by the Constitution and laws of the United States." Website topics include voting rights, free speech, national security, racial justice, and more

American Constitution Society
1899 L Street NW, Suite 200
Washington, DC 20036
(202) 393-6181
email: info@ACSLaw.org
website: www.acslaw.org
ACS is a progressive legal organization in the United States with more than 200 chapters. The ACS says it "dedicates itself to advancing and defending democracy, justice, equality, and liberty; to securing a government that serves the public interest; and to guarding against the abuse of law and the concentration of power."

Center for American Progress
1333 H Street NW, 10th Floor
Washington, DC 20005
(202) 682-1611
contact form: www.americanprogress.org/about/contact-us
website: www.americanprogress.org
The Center for American Progress is an independent, nonpartisan policy institute dedicated to "improving the lives of all Americans, through bold, progressive ideas."

Citizens for Responsibility and Ethics in Washington (CREW)
1101 K Street NW, Suite 201
Washington, DC 20005
(202) 408-5565
website: www.citizensforethics.org
email: info@citizensforethics.org
CREW is a nonprofit organization that "fights abuses of power and violations of the law" through research, communications, and legal action. The "What's New" page discusses current events in politics.

Liberty Fund
11301 N. Meridian Street
Carmel, IN 46032-4564
(800) 866-3520
email: info@libertyfund.org
website: www.libertyfund.org
Liberty Fund is dedicated to the "preservation, restoration, and development of individual liberty through investigation, research, and educational activity." Read essays and blog posts, hear podcasts, or browse its scholarly books on liberty in law and economics.

National Constitution Center
Independence Mall
525 Arch Street
Philadelphia, PA 19106
(215) 409-6600
contact form: constitutioncenter.org/about/contact
website: constitutioncenter.org
"The National Constitution Center unites America's leading scholars from diverse legal and philosophical perspectives to explore the text, history, and meaning of the US Constitution." Check out the Interactive Constitution to see how experts agree and disagree about history and to explore arguments about constitutional debates.

Poynter Institute
801 Third Street South
St. Petersburg, FL 33701
(727) 821-9494
website: poynter.org
email: info@newsu.org
The Poynter Institute for Media Studies is a nonprofit journalism school and research organization. "Poynter champions freedom of expression, civil dialogue and compelling journalism that helps citizens participate in healthy democracies." Sign up for newsletters or learn about fact checking.

Project on Government Oversight (POGO)
1100 G Street NW, Suite 500
Washington, DC 20005-7433
(202) 347-1122
email: info@pogo.org
website: www.pogo.org
POGO is a nonpartisan, independent watchdog that investigates waste, corruption, and abuse of power in the government. "We champion reforms to achieve a more effective, ethical, and accountable federal government that safeguards constitutional principles." Check out analysis on topics such as constitutional principles.

Supreme Court of the United States
1 First Street NE
Washington, DC 20543
(202) 479-3000
contact form: https://www.supremecourt.gov/contact/contact_pio.aspx
website: www.supremecourt.gov
Learn about the US Supreme Court, current justices, and how the Court works. The website also provides case documents, arguments, and opinions from Court cases.

For Further Reading

Books

Begala, Paul. *You're Fired: The Perfect Guide to Beating Donald Trump*. New York, NY: Simon & Schuster, 2020. A political expert discusses "the lessons we can learn from the [Republican] party's successes and failures."

Bowman, Frank O., III. *High Crimes and Misdemeanors: A History of Impeachment for the Age of Trump*. Cambridge, UK: Cambridge University Press, 2019. A constitutional scholar combines a deep historical and constitutional analysis of the impeachment clauses, a theory of when impeachment should be used, and a presentation of the case for and against impeachment of President Trump.

Cohen, Adam. *Supreme Inequality: The Supreme Court's Fifty-Year Battle for a More Unjust America*. London, UK: Penguin Press, 2020. The author "surveys the most significant Supreme Court rulings since the Nixon era and exposes how rarely the Court has veered away from its agenda of promoting inequality."

Dershowitz, Alan. *Defending the Constitution: Alan Dershowitz's Senate Argument Against Impeachment*. New York, NY: Hot Books, 2020. A legal scholar made an impassioned argument before the US Senate against the impeachment of Donald Trump. That argument is explored here.

Lamb, Charles M., and Jacob R. Neiheisel. *Presidential Leadership and the Trump Presidency: Executive Power and Democratic Government* (The Evolving American Presidency). London, UK: Palgrave Macmillan, 2020. Seven presidential politics scholars address important topics, including "presidential leadership theory and the Trump presidency, examining its mistruths, analyzing its record in the lower federal courts, probing its use of the pardon power, debating whether it requires an entirely new United States constitution to prevent future authoritarian threats."

McHale, Tom. *The Practical Guide to the United States Constitution: A Historically Accurate and Entertaining Owners' Manual for the Founding Documents*. Chicago, IL: IPG, 2018. This book's mission is "to make the Constitution so easy to understand that even a career politician can grasp it."

Raphael, Ray. *The US Constitution: Explained for Every American*. New York, NY: Vintage, 2017. Historian and Constitutional expert Ray Raphael guides readers through the origins, impact, and current relevance of the Constitution, including the amendments.

Rozell, Mark J., and Mitchel A. Sollenberger. *Executive Privilege: Presidential Power, Secrecy, and Accountability* (Studies in Government and Public Policy). Lawrence, KS: University Press of Kansas, 2020. An in-depth history and analysis of executive privilege. This title explores the proper scope and limits of presidential power.

Skousen, Paul B., and Mrs. W. Cleon Skousen. *How to Read the Constitution and the Declaration of Independence: A Simple Guide to Understanding the Constitution of the United States* (Freedom in America Book 1). Salt Lake City, UT: Izzard Ink Publishing, 2016. This "easy, step-by-step guide" includes visual tools, exercises, and several memory aids to help readers understand the Constitution and the Declaration of Independence.

Periodicals and Internet Sources

Blackman, Josh. "President Obama, Meet the 'Take Care' Clause," *National Review*, January 20, 2016. https://www.nationalreview.com/2016/01/obama-dapa-supreme-court/

Calabrese, Chris. "When Presidents Use Executive Privilege," *Constitution Daily*, March 24, 2017. https://constitutioncenter.org/blog/when-presidents-use-executive-privilege

Denniston, Lyle. "Constitution Check: What Does the 'Take Care Clause' Mean?" *Constitution Daily*, February 4, 2016. https://constitutioncenter.org/blog/constitution-check-what-does-the-take-care-clause-mean/

Driesen, David M. "Executive Privilege and Impeachment," American Constitution Society, October 3, 2019. https://www.acslaw.org/expertforum/executive-privilege-and-impeachment/

Franklin, Dan. "Evolution of the Principle of Executive Privilege," Encyclopaedia Britannica, Inc., 2020. https://www.britannica.com/topic/executive-privilege

Frum, David. "Heads, Trump Wins. Tails, We All Lose," *Atlantic*, November 26, 2019. https://www.theatlantic.com /ideas/archive/2019/11/trump-absolute-immunity -and-supreme-court/602665/

Herzig, David. "President Trump and Tax Return Privacy," *Forbes*, April 5, 2018. https://www.forbes.com/sites/davidherzig/2018/04/05 /president-trump-and-tax-return-privacy/#606c52f4595e

Jacobson, Louis. "What You Need to Know About Executive Privilege," PolitiFact, May 8, 2019. https://www.politifact.com/article/2019/may/08/what-you-need-know-about-executive -privilege/

Marshall, William P. "Article II, Section 3 and the Limits of Presidential Power," National Constitution Center. https:// constitutioncenter.org/interactive-constitution/interpretation /article-ii/clauses/348#article-ii-section-3-by-bill-marshall

Martin, Michel, and Mark Rozell. "Trump and the Parameters of Executive Privilege," NPR, March 3, 2018. https://www.npr .org/2018/03/03/590616771/trump-and-the-parameters-of -executive-privilege

Mulligan, Katrina, and Aminata Diallo. "The Executive Privilege Is Far from Absolute," Center for American Progress, October 16, 2019. https://www.americanprogress.org/issues/security /news/2019/10/16/475900/executive-privilege-far-absolute/

Neuman, Scott. "Executive Privilege: A Long (And Sometimes Sordid) History," NPR, June 20, 2012. https://www.npr.org /sections/itsallpolitics/2012/06/20/155442846/executive -privilege-a-long-and-sometimes-sordid-history

Rosenberg, Mort. "The Limits of Executive Privilege," POGO, May 15, 2019. https://www.pogo.org/report/2019/05/the-limits-of -executive-privilege/

Rozell, Mark J. "The Constitution and Executive Privilege," Law & Liberty, July 12, 2012. https://www.lawliberty.org/2012/07/12/the -constitution-and-executive-privilege/

Shafer, Ronald G. "'Not Above the Law': Executive Privilege's Contentious History from Washington to Trump," *Washington Post*, June 12, 2019. https://www.washingtonpost.com/history/2019/06/12

/not-above-law-executive-privileges-contentious-history
-washington-trump/

Shaub, Jonathan. "Executive Privilege Should Have No Power When It Comes to an Impeachment," *Atlantic*, November 15, 2019. https://www.theatlantic.com/ideas/archive/2019/11/no-executive-privilege-in-impeachment/602044

Shaub, Jonathan. "The Executive's Privilege: Rethinking the President's Power to Withhold Information," Lawfare, October 31, 2019. https://www.lawfareblog.com/executives-privilege-rethinking-presidents-power-withhold-information

Smith, Glenn. "Just How Privileged? (Five Key Points About Executive Privilege)," SDSU World Campus, 2015, 2017, 2019. https://ces.sdsu.edu/sites/default/files/cc13-justhowprivileged.pdf

UShistory.org. "The Evolution of the Presidency." https://www.ushistory.org/gov/7a.asp

Vladeck, Steve. "Executive Privilege, Congress' Subpoena Power, and the Courts: A Brief Overview of a Complex Topic," SCOTUSblog, October 16, 2019. https://www.scotusblog.com/2019/10/executive-privilege-congress-subpoena-power-and-the-courts-a-brief-overview-of-a-complex-topic/

Waxman, Olivia B. "President Trump Invoked Executive Privilege. Here's the History of That Presidential Power," *Time*, June 13, 2019. https://time.com/5605930/executive-privilege-history/

Wolf, Zach. "Why Trump's Claim of Executive Privilege Is Different," CNN, May 8, 2019. https://www.cnn.com/2019/05/08/politics/donald-trump-executive-privilege/index.html

Websites

Independence Hall Association (www.ushistory.org)
The IHA provides online resources on US history from the precolonial era to the present. Find historic documents and free online textbooks for high school courses in US history and American government.

Lawfare (www.lawfareblog.com)

Lawfare is a blog dedicated to national security issues. It provides essays on topics such as homeland security, surveillance, war powers, and foreign policy.

National Review (www.nationalreview.com)

National Review is a conservative opinion magazine. It includes articles on law and economics from a Republican conservative perspective.

The Progressive (progressive.org)

The Progressive aims to "amplify voices of dissent and those under-represented in the mainstream, with a goal of championing grassroots progressive politics." Read articles and opinion pieces, or learn about its op-ed writing clinics.

SCOTUSblog (www.scotusblog.com)

This law blog is written by lawyers, law professors, and law students. The site tracks cases before the Supreme Court of the United States.

Index

Picture Credits